Frederick Pollock

The land laws

Frederick Pollock

The land laws

ISBN/EAN: 9783337232870

Printed in Europe, USA, Canada, Australia, Japan

Cover: Foto ©Suzi / pixelio.de

More available books at **www.hansebooks.com**

WILLELMO . STVBBS

COLLEGAE . COLLEGA

MAGISTRO . DISCIPVLVS

HAEC . QVANTVLACVNQVE

D.D.D.

PREFACE TO THE THIRD EDITION

The object of this book, as I formerly defined it, is to make the principles and the leading features of the English law of real property intelligible to a reader who is without legal training, but is willing to take some little pains to understand. It does not aim at being a practical manual, and therefore many things that take an important place in counsel's chambers and the solicitor's office, such as the Conveyancing Acts and the Settled Land Acts, are purposely treated with great brevity. Collateral topics such as local taxation, death duties, and game laws, were and are omitted simply because there was no room for them.

Research has done much to the history of the law, and legislation to the modern law itself, in the eight years that have passed since the second edition was issued. The present revision is, for divers reasons, less thoroughgoing than I could have wished; but I trust that few serious errors remain, and that no recent statutes of general importance have been overlooked. I have found it necessary to rewrite a good deal of the chapter on early customary law, to alter much of the Appendix, and to add a wholly new note on the Origins of the Manor, in order to keep the antiquarian part abreast of the present state of scholarship. Perhaps we do not know much more about the Anglo-Saxon period than we did a dozen years ago (except that on some points we really know less than we supposed); but of the Anglo-Norman and Angevin periods—thanks to Mr. Seebohm, Mr. Vinogradoff, Mr. Maitland, Mr. Round, and Dr. Liebermann—we do know a good deal more both positively and negatively.

At some points I have now ventured to refer for proofs or details to the *History of English Law before the Time of Edward I.*, lately published by Mr. Maitland and myself.

The dedication to the Bishop of Oxford remains in its original form in memory of the too short time for which I had the honour to be his colleague as a professor in the University.   F. P.

CONTENTS

CHAPTER VI

CHAPTER VII

APPENDIX

CHAPTER I

The laws and usages which govern the tenure of land in England are, as a whole, unique. Our land system is commonly called feudal, sometimes by persons who use the word as a disparaging epithet without any clear notion of what it means. This is not in itself wrong, but it conveys a most imperfect notion of the number and variety of the influences that have made our land laws what they are. The statement and the belief implied in it are so inadequate as to be misleading. Almost every possible kind of ownership, and almost every possible relation of owners and occupiers of land to the State and to one another, have at one time or another existed in England, and left a more or less conspicuous mark in the composite structure of the English law of real property. We have to follow out a long story before we can understand how much and how little feudalism abides in the present state of things. There are still in force many local customs and rights which are now known to date—in their nature in all cases, and in their actual origin in many—from a time

when the feudal system was unheard of, and indeed
when private property in land, as we now understand
it, was a struggling novelty. The main body of the
technical expressions of the law, and of the technical
habit of thought which they preserve, is derived from
feudalism; but this feudalism has been deeply modified
by circumstances peculiar to England. In Scotland the
feudal system grew to its full development with little
interference, if any, from legislation; and the forms of
Scottish land law still preserve the system in great comparative purity. Here legislation has constantly inter-
fered, and its effects have been to produce radical
changes. These changes have not always been such as
the Legislature intended; in one or two material in-
stances the effect has been the very opposite of that
which was aimed at. One celebrated measure of
Henry VIII.'s reign, the Statute of Uses, was passed in
order to restore the ancient simplicity and notoriety of
titles to land, though more in the interest of the Crown
and other great lords than in that of the public. The
object of the statute was before long defeated by
judicial construction. But it did not remain inoperative; it had other and quite unexpected results. The
first was to make the transfer of land, without any act
or ceremony for securing publicity, far easier than it
had ever been before. The second, worked out in the
days of the Commonwealth and the Restoration by the
ingenuity of two or three lawyers, was to introduce the
method of strict settlement of landed property which
is practised by a great proportion of landowners to this
day. Thus, as we shall see more fully hereafter, a
measure intended to compel notoriety and simplicity

became the chief instrument of secrecy and complication. Turning, on the other hand, from the titles and tenures of owners to the relation between owners and occupiers, we find this resting to a great extent on something thoroughly opposed to feudal ideas—namely, the modern economical conception of land as an article of commerce which, like any other commodity, is bought, sold, and hired for prices regulated by competition. In the case of town dwelling-houses, and buildings used for trade or manufacture, this view is carried out to its full extent, and the relation between landlord and tenant is a purely commercial one. As to farm-holdings, it is still otherwise in most cases, owing to the survival of usages and habits which we may in a loose way call feudal if we please.

Thus our system of landed property is a structure of the most complex and heterogeneous kind. So great is the technical complication and difficulty of our laws on the subject, that within the special studies of the legal profession the study of them is a speciality of itself. Even among accomplished lawyers the number of those who are well versed in real property law is but small; the number of those who know the history of the law is a smaller one still. Forty or fifty years ago learned persons might be found, such as the late Lord St. Leonards, who seriously maintained that this complication was inevitable, and was indeed only a mark of perfection in the machinery. Few persons, if any, can be found to maintain it now. But this very complication which calls for amendment is one of the chief obstacles in the way of amendment being made. The whole subject is such a mystery to laymen that, though they may know something is amiss, they cannot tell where the remedy should begin, and do not know what to ask for. Among lawyers a considerable number are hostile to change, and a greater number indifferent. Those who make the shoe do not feel it pinch, and those who feel it pinch do not know how shoes are made. It has often been said that in no country are landowners so ignorant of their legal position or so dependent on legal advice as in England; and I believe it cannot be contradicted. A century or two ago country gentlemen commonly had some little knowledge of the law of property; three centuries ago they had a good deal, as we may learn from Shakespeare; now they seldom have any unless they have practised at the Bar. It would seem, therefore, worth a serious effort to overcome or break down in some fashion the barrier between the minds of lawyers and laymen which is apt to make discussion between them a game of cross purposes. How this can best be brought about is a knotty question. Statements made in the proper technical terms are in danger of not being understood, or, what is worse, being misunderstood; while for those who are once accustomed to the use of such terms it is far from easy to state the same facts, even in the most general outlines, in language to be understood by all men, and yet accurate as far as it goes. One common method of popular exposition, not only in law but in other special sciences, is to give loose or insufficient explanations of the terms of art, and then use the terms as if the reader had been enabled really to understand them. This is the most dangerous way of all, being by so much worse than those which lead to mere bewilderment as false know-

ledge is worse than ignorance. Instruction of this kind
is answerable, presumably, for the loose talk about
primogeniture and entail which still abounds in the
mouths of people who might easily know better.
Serious and capable writers, Mr. George Brodrick and
some others, have done something to provide a remedy.
But the discussion of economical questions has left
them, as a rule, hardly room enough to show clearly
and plainly the legal composition of our land system.
Now the whole structure, as we have just said, and as
Mr. Brodrick points out in a notable passage of his
book, is a result of many successive accretions, and
those not of a natural but of a casual sort. It has not
been produced by deliberate legislation, nor yet by the
spontaneous growth of custom. Hence it cannot be
understood by itself. It has no intrinsic coherence,
and no organic principles. It is a series of historical
accidents, and becomes intelligible only in the light of
its historical conditions. And this is not less the case,
but rather the more so, when the persons desiring to
understand it are viewing it from the outside and are
unfamiliar with its details. Our aim therefore will be,
so far as our skill reaches and the thing can be done on
so small a scale, to disentangle the several historical
elements that go to make up our modern English real
property law.

Let us imagine ourselves placed on some commanding
point within the boundaries of a great English estate,
looking over its mansion-house and its park, its fields
and pastures, its woods and wastes. Over against us
there rises an open hill, covered, it may be, with brilliant gorse and heather in their season, and fringed and

crested with wild woods. These are open and common
lands, over which many persons have rights of putting
so many beasts to graze, of cutting turf and underwood
for the use of their habitations, and the like, according
to the custom of the country and place. Such rights
were explained by our law-books, until quite recently,
so as to make them fit into a complete feudal theory
of land-holding. They were supposed to have been
granted by the lord of the manor to his tenants, or to
have grown up within his domain by way of sufferance
and usage, till the long-continued approval of successive
lords passed from a matter of favour into a matter of
right. This, or something like it, may sometimes have
happened. But in general the true history is just the
other way. The people who exercise rights of common
exercise them by a title which, if we could only trace it
all the way back, is far more ancient than the lord's.
Their rights are such as belonged to the members of a
township or agricultural community long before the legal
theory of manors and lords of the manor was heard of.
Perhaps there are also parcels of Lammas land in the
neighbourhood—fields which are enclosed and cultivated
part of the year, and during the other part thrown
open for the common use of the several occupiers, or
(as is more likely to be the case) of a larger class of
persons. Such arrangements are relics of the time
when separate ownership of land was in its infancy.
Those and other ancient communal rights are often
vested in the inhabitants of the parish, which may well
be thought to represent a still older community, and to
preserve in such lingering usages some traces of its
original constitution. Examples of them have been

much diminished in the last few generations by the steady progress of enclosures, but they are still not uncommon. Between our imagined past and the waste land there lies a stretch of cultivated ground, occupied by one or more farmers. They may hold under leases for a considerable term of years, or only from year to year, but in the latter case they may, under favourable circumstances, enjoy a good deal of practical security in their tenure.[1] In any case their legal condition is of a relatively modern and simple kind. It was barely provided for in the economy of the feudal system, and is exempt from the mysteries of the law of real property. A leaseholder's interest in his farm is dealt with, in case of his death without disposing of it by will, in exactly the same way as his interest in the stock on the farm, or money in the funds, or any other movable property. In the language of the law it is *personal*, and not *real* estate. The complexities of which we have spoken affect him only through his landlord, in so far as they tie the landlord's hands in dealing with the tenant and improving the property. Nearer to us, again, at the foot of the park, is a little home-farm, kept in hand and managed by an agent on the lord's immediate behalf. This method of cultivation was the prevailing one for a considerable part of the Middle Ages. We now meet with it in England only as an exception; sometimes it is a luxury, sometimes an experiment, sometimes the necessity of a bad season.

Now let us turn to the park and the manor-house

---

[1] During the recent and unhappily continuing period of depression the difficulty has been much oftener for landlords to keep their tenants.

itself, which may fill the foreground of our imaginary
landscape. The lord of all this is himself a tenant,
though not in the popular sense, or to much practical
effect. His lands are held of the Crown, or perhaps of
some other superior who himself holds of the Crown.
His predecessors before the Commonwealth time owed
rent or services, or both, and were subject to a variety
of occasional dues and payments, some of them of a
vexatious kind. They were bound to follow the king
or other over-lord when he went forth to war, and
bring with them a specified armed force, or pay for the
maintenance of its equivalent. The feudal dues and
services have been abolished; but ancient money-rents,
technically known by various names, and reduced to a
nominal amount by the changes that have taken place in
the standard of the coinage and the value of the precious
metals, often survive to this day. Some ancient rents
are not in money but in kind. The city of London still
pays to the Crown certain horse-shoes and nails as the
rent of a piece of land in the parish of St. Clement Danes,
once granted by the king to a farrier, and a faggot as
the rent of some waste lands in Shropshire.[1] In some
cases the Crown is entitled to receive some weapon of
war, or part of warlike equipment—a sword, a banner,
a pair of gloves, or spurs. Once or twice these ancient
tenures, which were esteemed peculiarly honourable,
have been imitated in modern times on the occasion of
public grants for distinguished military services. But

---

[1] These rents are now received by the Queen's Remembrancer a
few days before the beginning of Michaelmas term. The payment
has for more than 150 years become merely ceremonial, the same
horse-shoes and nails, preserved in the Queen's Remembrancer's
office, doing duty on each occasion.

if the remnant of feudal relations to a superior is at this
day no burden to the English landowner, and at most
adds a picturesque circumstance to his title, he is apt to
be restrained in other ways of more modern and subtle
invention. The lord of this mansion is named by all
men its owner; it is said to belong to him: the park,
the demesne, the farms, are called his. But we shall be
almost safe in assuming that he is not the full and free
owner of any part of it. He is a "limited owner," having an interest only for his own life. He might have
become the full owner, though still under a greater or
less burden of encumbrances created by his predecessors,
if he had possessed the means of waiting, the independ-
ence of thought and will to break with the tradition of
his order and the bias of his education, and the energy
to persevere in his dissent against the counsels and feel-
ings of his family. But he has had every inducement to
let things go their accustomed way. Those whom he
had always trusted told him, and probably with sincere
belief, that the accustomed way was the best for the
family, for the land, for the tenants, and for the country.
And there could be no doubt that it was at the time the
most agreeable to himself. As soon, or almost as soon,
as he was of age to bind himself, he entered into a new
settlement, by which his own interest was reduced, like
his father's before him, to that of a life-tenant, and the
succession of his offspring secured in advance down to
the furthest limits allowed by the law. The legal
machinery by which this is done is little more than two
centuries old, and, though refined and improved in details
by the ingenuity of generations of conveyancers, has not
been much altered in substance since its first invention.

It owes nothing to legislation, except by accident. Thus, then, the apparent owner of the domain is no more absolute as to its actual disposition and management than the king is absolute in a limited monarchy. He can do but little of his own motion, and what he does is for the benefit of successors not of his own choice. Likely enough, he has no clear notion of his own powers and their limits. An English family settlement is on the whole less intelligible, and certainly less understood by most English citizens, than the English Constitution. In practice the limited owner has to put himself a good deal in the hands of experts, and oftentimes he is fain to make the family solicitor his prime minister. The advice he gets is pretty sure to be on the safe side—that is, on the side of not trying experiments. A family solicitor, unlike those who administer affairs of State, has no motive whatever for being enterprising in his client's affairs, and many to the contrary. He cannot hurt himself by over-caution, and may hurt himself much by rashness. So he takes, as a rule, the line of doing as little as possible, which is one much commended in all walks of life to those whose first object is their own peace and quietness.

Peradventure the lord of this estate is lord in a strict legal sense—that is, as lord of a manor. We have, indeed, assumed as much in our description. In this capacity he is a kind of small sovereign prince, possessed of his own courts, and doing justice according to his own procedure and customs. But his powers and jurisdiction are shrivelled by the changes and chances of centuries into next to nothingness, and only the names of them remain. In the voluminous settlement which confers title to these lands on him and his issue, the manorial

franchises are enumerated in a roll of strange-looking
terms, many of which are now obscure even to the
lawyer, unless he is also a historical student; there are
English words among them of immemorial antiquity,
which had their technical meaning centuries before the
Conquest, and which the Norman lawyers, only half
understanding them, thought it prudent to leave un-
translated. They hold their own through the invasion
of Norman-French and Latin, and their native English
hardly knows them again when it meets them. As for
the lord himself, he knows neither the words nor their
meaning unless he happens to be a scholar and an
antiquary. Nor is he concerned to know them for any
purpose of business. The ancient franchises and profits
are obsolete, and have been so for many generations.
The manorial courts exist in form, and their records are
kept in the ancient fashion. But the fine by which a
thief caught within the boundaries redeemed his life is
no longer a source of revenue to the manor, neither does
the lordship of "view of frankpledge and all that to view
of frankpledge doth belong" convey any sensible increase
to the wealth or the dignity of the modern landowner.
To be lord of a manor is to be the lord of a secular ruin,
in which he that knows the secret of the crabbed spell-
book may call up the ghosts of a vanished order of the
world.

Thus we have taken a hasty view of the legal aspects
of an English landed estate, which will presently come
before us one by one for a more detailed survey. It is
an unparalleled accumulation of layer upon layer of
diverse materials. Tenure and convention, custom and
competition, legislation and usage, the rude common

life of the free Teutonic warrior tribes, an aristocratic
military system sprung from sheer necessities of mutual
defence, and disguised in the terms and reasons of a
Romanised law, the subtle deductions of a legal profession trained in scholastic disputes, the attempts of an
impatient Parliament to make their crooked things
straight, the not less subtle and more flexible inventions
of modern lawyers, the partial clearances and half-
hearted amendments of modern law-reformers : all these
have gone to the making of the vast and inextricable
mass, and all must be considered in their turn by the
seeker who is bold enough to search out the history and
the meaning of the land laws of England.

It may be not amiss, meanwhile, to point out one or
two of the general features in which the legal concep-
tions of ownership and rights over land are at variance
with the popular ones. It is commonly supposed that
land belongs to its owner in the same sense as money or
a watch. This has not been the theory of English law
since the Norman Conquest, nor has it been so, in its
full significance, at any time. No absolute ownership of
land is recognised by our law-books except in the Crown.
All lands are supposed to be held, immediately, or mediately, of the Crown, though no rent or services may be
payable, and no grant from the Crown on record. The
feudal lawyers forestalled to some extent in substance,
and to a large extent in form, the modern Socialist
dream of the State as the universal landlord. On the
other hand, the law is equally far from countenancing
the belief that there is land which belongs to nobody
and is free to all the world. Some such belief is
probably held by most people who are not lawyers.

Appearances are certainly in its favour, and indeed the thing was legally possible in the Roman system, and I suppose is still legally possible in many Continental countries. But in England it is not legally possible. Land may be subject to public rights of way, to rights of common, and to a great variety of private rights. It may be worthless for all purposes except those of recreation, and the owner may be undiscoverable. But an owner there must be somewhere; the Crown in the last resort if no other is forthcoming. I am not aware that the public at large have a strict right to be anywhere except on highways (including estuaries and navigable rivers) and public paths, in places expressly dedicated to public use and enjoyment by their former owners or by Act of Parliament, and on the foreshore of the sea between high and low water-mark. And, strictly speaking, the right to be even on a highway is limited to the purpose of passing and repassing. As Whewell, when he was still only a tutor of Trinity College, Cambridge, said of the College bridge over the Cam, it is a place of transit and not of lounge. In like manner the right to be on the foreshore is of doubtful extent. It is said to be limited to purposes connected with navigation and fishery, though this opinion was given not without weighty protest, and would perhaps not be upheld now. There is a widely-spread popular notion that the public have the right of going not merely along the foreshore, but along the edge of the cliff, where by reason of the steepness of the coast there is no foreshore; in short, that it is of common right to make one's way along the coast somehow, by the foreshore where there is any, but if not, then other-

wise. So far as I can discover, there is no legal
authority whatever for this belief. We may take the
legal contrast between Wimbledon Common and Dartmoor as another pretty striking illustration. To ordinary observation they both have the air of waste places
belonging to nobody, and Dartmoor, I need hardly say,
is much the waster and wilder of the two. A shrewd
observer might guess from the situation of Wimbledon
Common that it would hardly remain open at this day
if something had not been done to preserve it. But
certainly no one but a lawyer would guess that the
public have a better right to be on Wimbledon Common
than on Dartmoor. Yet such is the case. Wimbledon
Common has been dedicated to the public by an Act of
Parliament. Dartmoor is, in practice, quite as free
for all the world to walk and ride on, but the number
of persons who have any strict right to be there is
probably by no means a large one. Most of the moor
belongs to the Duchy of Cornwall, which, on the whole,
is better for the public than if it belonged to private
owners. The only legal obstacle to Dartmoor being
enclosed is the existence of rights of pasture and turf-
cutting over it, which, of course, belong not to the
public but to a definite though considerable number of
commoners. Probably it might be found in the case of
Dartmoor, as in the case of Epping, that the old forest
laws afford means which may at this day be used with
effect against encroachments, but still the public at
large would have no enforceable right.[1] The same is

---

[1] The customs of Dartmoor have never been thoroughly investi-
gated, and the materials are still only in part accessible. There
is every reason to believe that the result would be most interest-

the case with any other common which is not preserved by statute. Practically the unenclosed and untilled ground of England is free to the public for two reasons. The owners have no interest in keeping the public off, and would find it both an invidious and a troublesome thing if they tried. Against a trespasser not in pursuit of game the only remedy is a civil action, and no jury would give substantial damages, nor any judge give costs, against a trespasser on a wild moor or down who had neither molested the owner, disputed his title, nor injured his property. No one is likely to spend his money for the sake of having a farthing damages, being told by the judge that it serves him right, and making himself odious and ridiculous. As a rule we hear of actions for trespass only when there is a claim of right to be settled. This is an example of a principle that runs through the whole administration of law, and in English law is very conspicuous. It is impossible so to limit the rights of owners that they cannot sometimes be harshly and vexatiously used. But it is possible to have things so ordered that the extreme use of a man's legal rights which would be intolerable to his neighbours shall also give to himself so much trouble as will deter most men from attempting it. This is accomplished in England partly by an active public opinion, partly by the wide discretion entrusted to judges and juries. For many things of great importance, including all the modern developments of the British Constitution, we

ing. The Dartmoor Preservation Association has done what it could with the means at its disposal; see Mr. Elton's article in *Law Quart. Rev.* vi. 207 (the volume there noticed was issued only to members).

are content to rely on understandings rather than positive law. The day may come when express law has to take the place of these informal understandings. It has come in the business of Parliament, in the relations between landlords and farmers, in the matter of labourers' allotments, and in many matters of local government. It is useless to deprecate changes of this kind in the face of need; but there will always be a sort of people, often the best sort, who regret the old easy-going ways.

It may seem strange that in England, the land where above all others the personal and political rights of the simplest freeman have been saved whole through all changes of princes and dynasties, the law should find so little room for public and unstinted rights of using the very elements. Even the air is not free, for the maxim is that the owner of the soil is owner up to the height above and down to the depth beneath. It seems to be the law that to pass over land in a balloon, at whatever height, without the owner's or occupier's licence, is technically a trespass. This doctrine does not, for the reasons I have mentioned, lead to any grave inconvenience. If it did, its historical explanation would not throw much light on the question of what should be done with it, much less justify its continuance. But the explanation is not far to seek, and it is fitting that we should put ourselves in a position, so far as we can, to judge ancient institutions and maxims with all fairness, not only as to their present convenience for us, but as to their origin and history, and the reasons of their acceptance in the past. In this case history tells us that the conception of rights common

to all the public is a modern one. Even the personal
freedom of the old days was the right of a privileged
class, for below the freeman there were unfree men,
serfs bound to the soil and slaves, the conquered foes
of past generations and the captives of his own. The
Roman citizenship, which had grown step by step from
the exclusive franchise of a conquering tribe to the
common right of every freeman in the empire, had its
community rudely broken up by the Teutonic invasions.
Far into the Middle Ages law was for many purposes
not general or territorial, but personal. Besides the
radical distinction between free and unfree men, the
freeman of the Carolingian empire might be a Frank,
or a Lombard, or a Roman provincial, and in every case
he would be governed by a different law. So in
British India to this day there are widely different laws
of marriage and inheritance for the Hindu, the Mussul-
man, and the Parsee, and sensibly different laws, though
not so different, for the Hindus of Bengal and the
Hindus of Madras. In Europe this kind of difference
could not persist. The victory of the Christian Church,
and the revival of the Roman ideal of uniformity, which
had first moulded her institutions and then found a
last refuge in them, destroyed all personal distinctions
founded on religion by making the Church include the
State.[1] Distinctions founded on race went the same

[1] As late as Coke's time it was the theory of English lawyers
that an infidel or pagan could have no civil rights. Jews certainly
had none before their expulsion by Edward I. Regulations were
made for their government, and they were ultimately banished
from the realm, by the sole authority of the Crown ; and they are
expressly called the king's serfs in contemporary documents. In
medieval theory no one not a Christian could be a real member of
the State, and Christianity was one and indivisible.

way ere long. The Norman and the Englishman, and
at a later day the Englishman and the Welshman, became one people. But a man's rights were still for the
most part his rights, not simply as an Englishman, but
as a member of some particular class and community.
He lived under customs and enjoyed franchises which
might be peculiar to his native town or even his native
parish.[1] In the Middle Ages there were few holders
of land, by however humble a tenure, who had not
some kind of rights of common annexed to their holdings. And every village and township would no doubt
be as anxious to exclude strangers from its woods and
pastures as to preserve its ordinary members' rights in
them against encroachment from within or from above.
We know, indeed, that the boundaries of the ancient
German communities were guarded by a kind of sacred
horror, and the most frightful penalties denounced upon
violators of the *mark*. The medieval Englishman's
rights of common provided for his wants both of use
and of recreation. People did not then travel for their
pleasure, or make recreation a study. The legal theory
which denied the possibility of public rights over land
was only the formal expression of the dispositions and
habits of society. These being what they were, the
usage by which popular rights are acquired could not
and did not grow up except within limited particular
regions, for particular purposes, and in the acts of small
local communities.

[1] Ample illustration of this may now be seen in Mrs. J. R.
Green's *The English Town in the Fifteenth Century*.

CHAPTER II

IT has been said that the most hopeful way to understand the present structure of our land laws may be to pick out separately the various elements which are now mingled in the mass. Let us begin with that which is the oldest, the most popular, and still in some respects the most persistent—I mean the customary Germanic law which our ancestors brought with them from the mainland on their first settlement in this country, and developed after their own fashion, with little substantial foreign interference or influence for good or for ill, until the reign of Edward the Confessor. Whatever else may be said of the early English land system, as preserved to us in Anglo-Saxon records and interpreted by modern scholars, it certainly had not the merit of simplicity. The modern law, though far from simple, is definite, and in the main uniform. Copyhold lands are subject to peculiar incidents and modes of alienation, and certain ancient varieties of tenure survive as local customs of inheritance. But with these exceptions, the substance of the law is the same for every piece of land in England. Before the Conquest there was no more one and the same law for every parcel of land than there was one and the same law for every man. Land, like men, was impressed with different legal qualities and conditions, though its condition was not unchangeable. Separate property in land was nothing new: in the time of Tacitus, the general truth of whose description there is no reason to doubt, every German freeman's homestead was already his own. Nevertheless full and free private ownership, as we now understand it, was an innovation, and for a long time exceptional, though its constant tendency was to encroach on the earlier forms of tenure.

Bócland, or book-land, is the regular term for land held in several property under the express terms of a written instrument, or book as it was then called. Such grants could be made in the first instance only by the king with the consent of his Witan. This tenure was of comparatively late introduction, and came in under the influence of the Church, and in favour of grants to religious houses. We will return to the details.

At this point we note that book-land is what we have most documents and authority about, for the simple reason that land held in any other way was not dealt with in writing, except occasionally in the wills of great persons.

We also read of folk-land. Far more has been written about this in modern times than the whole sum of our meagre authorities. There are only three places in Anglo-Saxon legal documents where the word occurs, and they enable us to say with absolute certainty only that folk-land was something contrasted with book-land. It seems to mean, as Spelman thought two centuries ago, land held by folk-right or customary law, as opposed

to land held by a written charter or "book." For
many years all or nearly all scholars, including myself,
accepted Allen's explanation that "folk-land" was *ager
publicus*, land held by the nation for public purposes.
But it has been shown by Mr. Vinogradoff[1] that this
brilliant and plausible interpretation really raised more
difficulties than it solved; and the restoration of Spelman's opinion has been accepted, so far as I know,
without an expression of dissent in any quarter.

Folk-land might belong either to the king as representing the State, or to the king for his private use,[2] or
to private persons; a good deal of it was also common
land used and enjoyed by the members of particular
townships, or sometimes perhaps larger bodies, to the
exclusion of strangers. To say that such land was the
property of the community whose members used it
would however be misleading; for the idea of a corporate
body being treated as a person, and having rights like
those of a natural person, was much too artificial for our
Germanic ancestors, I do not say merely to invent, but
to grasp when presented to them from Roman sources.
It made way with some difficulty even after the Norman
Conquest.[3] Early communal enjoyment is not an
artificial form of property, but one of the elements out
of which our developed notions of corporate existence
and corporate property have been made.

[1] *English Historical Review*, January 1893. In former editions
of the present work I pointed out some of the difficulties, and
suggested a partial explanation, which is now superseded by Mr.
Vinogradoff's simpler and completer method.
[2] This distinction may seem suspiciously modern. I can only
say that I think I find it in the documents.
[3] Pollock and Maitland, *Hist. Eng. Law*, i. 476 *sqq.*

Land held by individuals, whether in greater or in less quantity, was included in the general description of folk-land, unless it had been turned into book-land by a written grant or confirmation.

There is no reason to suppose that common lands were regularly the subject of alienation, or that there was any power to alienate them.[1] As to land held by individuals under local custom, very little is really known about it save what can be gathered by analogy from the customary tenures found surviving some centuries later, and from Continental laws and usage. Such land was sometimes dealt with by will; if it could be sold by the owner in his lifetime, it is not at all likely that before the Norman Conquest custom had anywhere reached the point of letting him do so without the consent of the family. Probably the stringency of the local customs varied from county to county and even from township to township.

Modern popular notions of "*heirland* that must perpetually descend from father to son"[2] may perhaps rather go back to these ancient customs of the country than to medieval entails under the statute *De Donis* (of which hereafter), unless indeed they are merely a confused apprehension of the practical effect of modern strict settlements. Alienation by sale or gift, so far as

[1] It is true that in Domesday, i. 213b, we read of Goldington in Bedfordshire, "Hanc terram tenuerunt homines villae communiter *et vendere potuerunt*." But this might have been purchased land. The express mention of the power of alienation tends to show that there was something exceptional. Taking the exceptions recorded in Domesday for rules has been a fruitful source of errors, as Mr. J. H. Round has lately pointed out.

[2] Joshua Williams, *Real Property*, 17th edition, 95.

it occurred at all, was no doubt executed by the archaic and popular forms of which traces may still be found in copyholds, and in which either actual or symbolical delivery of possession was a principal and essential feature.[1]

Book-land was coveted because it gave the holder something much more nearly approaching full ownership in the modern sense. The institution, it must be remembered, is not of home growth. It is taken over from ecclesiastical — in other words, from Roman, habits of mind. There were no limits to the power of disposal enjoyed by the owner of book-land, save those which might be laid upon him by the terms of the grant itself. According to those terms he could generally, without any further leave or consent, grant it in his lifetime, as he had received it, by *book*, or dispose of it by his will. We find a certain number of charters granting rights over common land, and sometimes apparently portions of the common land itself.[2] These rights must have been already annexed to the folk-land which is made into book-land by the charter. It may be that in some of these cases the grantees already held the land as an allotment of public or common land. They may well have had by custom some sort of right to a renewal of the allotment to themselves or their descendants. If this were so, the effect of the grant would be to confirm the customary title in perpetuity, and to release the land from most of the public dues and services to which land other than book-land was subject. The release of these burdens would require a regular grant from the king, with the

[1] See Note B in Appendix.
[2] References in Nasse, *Mittelalt. Feldgemeinschaft*, 17-22.

consent of the Witan, just as much as the severance of a new portion from the folk-land. This, however, is given only as a conjecture.

The contrast of book-land with folk-land does not mean that a grant of book-land destroyed existing inferior tenures or rights of occupancy. Doubtless it made no more difference to the actual occupiers and small owners who held by the customs of folk-land when a large tract was granted as book-land than it now makes to the tenant-farmers of a great estate when the freehold is sold or mortgaged, or to an occupying leaseholder in a city when there is a sale of the ground-rent. As now land may be held by a farmer on a lease made by a copyholder, while the freehold remains with the lord of the manor, so there is no difficulty in conceiving that the various kinds of interest in land known to Anglo-Saxon custom often co-existed in the same acres. The division is of rights and interests, not necessarily of boundaries.

It is evident from what has been said that the ultimate legal origin of book-land was always a grant made out of the folk-land. Ample records of such grants are preserved, and are, in fact, our chief means of knowledge as to the relation of book-land to folkland. The grant could be effectually made only by the king with the consent of the Witan, and also of his superior king, if he acknowledged any (for our records begin in a time when there were still many kings and under-kings of many tribes and kindreds of the English). Not only this consent was required for grants in perpetuity to private persons, but if the king wished to appropriate any part of the folk-land as his own heritage, a grant to himself had to be made out with the express sanction of his counsellors, in just the same form as if it had been to any other person.[1]   The notion that all public property was the king's, and that the king, on the other hand could not hold property like a private person, was formulated after the Conquest.   Yet we find somewhat earlier that when a man is forjudged of life and lands for cowardice in battle, as the lands held by him of a private lord go to that lord, so any book-land he may have is forfeit to the king, and, it would seem, at the king's personal disposal.[2]   In practice, however, it is at least possible that from a very early time much of the increase of book-land at the expense of folk-land took place in irregular ways.   It may often have been under colour of an occupation which was rightful in its origin, but as often, perhaps, by mere encroachment. The king and other great men had certain rights over the waste folk-land, and rights of use tended then, as much as they do now, to grow into claims of property in the hands of the strongest.   It fared with the unappropriated folk-land of the kingdom very much as it fared some centuries later, for similar reasons, with the common lands of the village or township which had

---

[1] It would seem that a grant of land was regularly made to the king by the Witan on his accession, for the support of his dignity during his reign: Cod. Dipl., 1312, Æthelred: "gratia dei me ad intelligibilem perducere dignata est ætatem, mihique per meorum optimatum decreta affluentem et copiosam terrarum largita est portionem." This charter, as well as Beda's well-known letter to Ecgbert (see next page), seems to point to the existence of a kind of public fund of land administered by the king and the Witan. Allen and his followers erred not in supposing that there was such land, but in taking folk-land to mean nothing else.

[2] Laws of Cnut, ii. 77.

become a manor. As early as the eighth century grants were made recklessly out of folk-land in the north of England to persons who professed the religious character merely to have the grant without the burden of the ordinary secular dues and services.[1] It seems also not unlikely that men of substance attempted to dispose of part of their folk-land as book-land, to pious uses or otherwise. It is certain that grants and wills of land described by the donors as book-land were not uncommonly disputed by their families, and that an ordinance of the Witan was thought needful to enforce even express prohibitions against alienation out of the family contained in the original "book."[2] The interests that were created in book-land by the original grants varied a good deal in their nature and duration. It is not known how far they were regulated by any fixed laws or usages. Sometimes a free and absolute power of disposal was conferred by the terms of the "book" on the person to whom the grant was made. Sometimes a special course of descent was prescribed, so that the disposition was analogous to a modern entail, or alienation was allowed only within the family.[3]

It is doubtful, however (as we see by the law of Alfred just cited), whether the will of the grantor was in such cases strictly observed in practice. A very common form was to grant an interest for one or more lives in succession, say to Oswine or Æthelwulf and to two heirs

[1] Beda, Letter to Ecgbert.

[2] *Laws of Alfred*, c. 41.

[3] Many examples of such limited gifts are collected in Kemble's Introduction to the *Codex Diplomaticus*. We may name as good specimens among charters No. 299, and among wills that of King Alfred, No. 314.

whomsoever he shall choose after his own time, with an ultimate gift to a religious house.

A grant of book-land on a large scale probably carried rights of private jurisdiction, but it did not create any new relation of tenure or jurisdiction between the king or other grantor and the grantee. Hence book land appeared to persons acquainted with Continental feudalism as not feudal but allodial, and "alodium" is the regular Latin equivalent of book-land in Anglo-Norman and late Anglo-Saxon documents. There is no trace of any English form of the word "alodium," still less is there any authority for applying the term to the private holdings of freemen which were not book-land. The word "ethel" was used by Kemble to denote such holdings, with "alod" as an alternative; but there is no authority whatever for either usage.[1]

Such was in its main outlines the Old-English system of land tenure. But we must not suppose that all or most of the actual occupiers and tillers of the soil held by any of the titles which we have enumerated. If we did, we should fall into the same mistake as a foreigner who in our own time should imagine from reading modern English law-books that the whole or the greater part of the present occupiers are freeholders. There was indeed nothing, or next to nothing, resembling even distantly in form our modern leases for years and other inferior tenancies.[2] Nor was there, as there has been ever since the thirteenth century,[3] any distinct class of labourers working on other people's land and paid by money

[1] Bishop Stubbs (*Const. Hist.* 3rd ed. 75, 76, *in notis*) had already observed this.

[2] But one grant for a fixed term of years is found in the whole of the *Codex Diplomaticus*, and that is for three years only.

[3] Vinogradoff, *Villainage in England*, 321.

wages. Nevertheless a great part of the cultivation of the land was undertaken by people who occupied it by the agreement or permission of the superior owner, and paid for its use in money, in kind, or in labour, not uncommonly in all three. Land thus held was known as _lǽn-land,_ and the tenant was said to hold it (literally to sit on it)[1] upon lǽn. The word, it is almost needless to add, is our modern _loan._ The lands of bishoprics and religious houses, in so far as they were not tilled by serfs belonging to the house and under its direct management, were dealt with in this manner; and we may well think that religious corporations had the chief hand in introducing lǽns, as they certainly had some centuries later with regard to leases of the modern type. The condition of the tenants of lǽn-land was various. The smallest of them were little better than cottiers; the largest may have been no worse than substantial farmers. Now and then they obtained a more permanent estate by grant from the owner, or as we should now say acquired the freehold. We have examples of a tenant of lǽn-land receiving a grant of his tenement by book, to hold it _for_ book-land as fully as he did for lǽn-land; and it appears to have been a well known practice for lords to make such grants to deserving tenants.[2]

---

[1] This phrase remained in use all through the Middle Ages. "Whosoever sitteth upon the ground of any man . . . the lord shall have an hariot of him as of another." (Customary of Tettenhall Regis, _ap._ Toulmin Smith, English Gilds, 432.) "The sitting" (as opposed to "quitting") "tenant" is a familar expression to this day.

[2] Kemble, _Saxons in England,_ i. 312, 313. As he says in the same place, "where there was lǽn, there could properly be no book"; but the use of terms was in practice more or less confused; for example, _Cod. Dipl.,_ 1062, where a grant by charter, indis-

This kind of tenancy was at first of minor importance. Towards the date of the Conquest, however, a great proportion of the actual occupiers must have held their lands on lǽn. In a certain sense it is even true to say that lǽn-land ultimately supplanted everything else, and that no other kind of landed property is recognised by the strict theory of modern English law. Historically, the growth of lǽn-land, and the changes thereupon consequent, are intimately connected with the personal relation of lord and man, of which, therefore, something must be said. It was familiar in England long before the Conquest, and constantly tended to assume greater importance in the constitution of society. At first it was confined to the small body of personal followers attached to the leaders of the Germanic tribes. At that time it was personal and nothing more, and there was no loss of rank or dignity on the follower's part. The chief's or king's companions must be free, and might be noble, and their service was an honour.[1] The modern European orders of nobility and knighthood owe to this aspect of the institution the greater part of their titles, their system, and their ceremonial; and European monarchies owe to it nearly all the pomp that surrounds

tinguishable in its nature and incidents from the regular type of grants for lives so made by religious houses, purports to be by way of lǽn (Ealferð biscop and ða higan on Wintaceastre habbað geláued [sic] hiora leófan friónd viii. hída landes on Eastune priora manna deg. etc.) The essence of lǽn, in any case, appears to have been holding under a definite person as superior by specific services. Possibly it was a following of the Gallo-Frankish precarium.

[1] Kemble's opinion that this relation involved the loss of freedom can only be called the eccentricity of a man of genius. It is disposed of by Konrad Maurer, Kritische Ueberschau, ii. 391 sqq.

them, and much of the sentiment on which their continuance depends. For many generations before the
Norman Conquest, as distinctions of rank and substance
between freemen increased, the old community of freemen, equal in personal condition if not in wealth, had
been virtually replaced by a ruling class with a humbler
and poorer multitude in dependence on them. For
some time this state of things had become associated
with the tenure of land to a considerable extent, and
had thus prepared the way for the feudal and manorial
system. Feudalism is the complete association of
territorial with personal dependence, and of both with
definite rights and duties of jurisdiction. The tenant
is not only an occupier who pays the owner in money
or in kind for the use of the land ; he owes him personal
service and allegiance and attendance at his court. The
lord himself may be in like manner bound to an over-
lord, and he again to another above him, until we come
to some one who holds of no lord, and who, in the
developed feudal theory, must be an absolutely sovereign
prince. Old English land law never reached this stage,
but it was tending towards it so fast that the Conquest
may be said to have only hastened its transformation.

As far as the personal relation is concerned, we find
it established in the earliest times of which we have any
trustworthy account. Every man was expected either
to be of substance enough to answer all payments he
might become liable for, whether to private suitors as
damages or composition, or to the public as fines, or to
be dependent on a lord who could answer for him.
Much as in English society of a far later time we find
"masterless men" to be a name of thieves, vagrants,

and peace-breakers, we find before the Conquest that no honest man can be without a lord unless he is a lord himself. In the first half of the tenth century this is fixed as a positive rule, and the lordless man must find a lord at his peril. If he or his kindred for him fail to do this, he becomes outlawed, and may be dealt with as a robber.[1] The men who had risen to the condition of being lords and protectors of the smaller freemen were naturally great or relatively great landowners. Their ancestors, we may suppose, had been distinguished by birth or exploits among their fellows, English or Danish, even before their settlement in this land. Enjoying at first a kind of undefined primacy among their equals, they gradually assumed a position of command. From the first, we may be pretty sure, their possessions were notably greater than those of common men, and gave them a corresponding influence on all public occasions. Each of them imitated the king to the best of his power by surrounding himself with a band of personal followers.[2] And the sorts of men likely to seek the personal service of a lord, or become dependent on him, were increased by several causes. The natural growth of population is one of these, for the land allotted in the first instance to the freemen of the conquering host would in a few generations be a too scanty means of livelihood for their descendants. Men with no secured possessions of their own were driven to find a place in dependence on those who had land and goods to spare.

[1] *Laws of Æthelstan*, ii. 2.

[2] It is a minor question whether there was any distinct condition or qualification for a private man entertaining followers, or in other words setting up as a lord. The better opinion appears to be that there was not.

Another large class of free dependents were those who had property, but were not strong enough to guard it in times of trouble. These commended themselves to a lord for protection, and with themselves their land. There were likewise the manumitted serfs, a class which became considerable in the tenth and eleventh centuries, manumission being encouraged by the Church and reckoned a pious work. Neither were the old motives wanting which in the time of Tacitus had led the young men of the German peoples to cast in their lot with kings and chiefs. Adventurers in search of warlike renown or booty, exiles driven from their home by civil strife, or flying the vengeance of a slain man's kindred, craftsmen skilled in the arts which supplied the luxuries and recreations of life, such as then they were;—all these still contributed to swell the number of dependents, as they had once chiefly formed it. So far the connection with land tenure appears as accidental. The companion may or may not be a landholder; and if he is, the lord to whom he is personally attached may or may not be his superior in respect of the land. On the other hand, we do not know, and have no right to assume, that the man who occupied another's land on lén was necessarily his personal dependent. In fact we find tenure and personal subordination or "commendation" separated even after the Conquest.[1] In course of time, however, and by steps of which the beginning may lie further back than the earliest of our documents, the dependent becomes a tenant, and at last dependency and tenancy become in legal theory co-extensive. According to the

---

[1] Examples are not infrequent in Domesday. See Round, *Feudal England*, 33.

tenant's degree of personal rank, the inchoate tenancy takes a different complexion. The personal aid and service rendered in war to the king and the earls by their more distinguished followers comes to be looked on as the equivalent of the benefits received by them. Even before the Conquest there are traces of duties and relations hardly distinguishable from the true military tenures of a later age. The free landowners owing military service to the king as chief of the nation are becoming tenants holding their lands by military service of the king as their personal lord.

Among the smaller folk things happened differently. Their hereditary holdings were generally, though we have no right to say always, under the common-field system of which the details have been made clear chiefly by Mr. Seebohm in late years.

We do not know that this system was regulated or enforced by any definite authority, and, as fragments of it have survived down to quite modern times without the help of any such authority,[1] we are not bound to

---

[1] In 1892 Mr. Aubrey Spencer reported to the Royal Commission on Labour that "in the village of Stratton" (in the Dorchester Poor Law Union) "there still exists an unenclosed arable field divided into 'livings' of about twenty acres each held upon lives." Rights of common for four cows and fifty sheep are attached to each "living." "It is, however, a striking fact that these small 'livings' are not as a rule cultivated by the owners themselves, but are principally let to two farmers who cultivate them with their own farms." In this case an open-field system appears to be completely detached from any manorial or other organisation capable of regulating it in any way, and has persisted, perhaps because of this detachment rather than in spite of it, long after it has ceased to be convenient to any one; cp. Mr. F. W. Maitland in Law Quart. Rev. ix. 224.

postulate a township court or administrative assembly
for that purpose in default of other evidence that
it existed.   All recent research points to the hundred,
not the township, being the lowest unit of judicial and
executive authority in the Anglo-Saxon period. The
origin of lords of the manor is to be sought in the
growth of personal dependence and private jurisdiction
rather than in any direct development of economic
relations.   It seems clear that we must put it back to
a remoter date than was implied, if not stated, in much
of the doctrine current when this book was first written.
The consolidation of the petty monarchy wielded in after-
times by the lord of the manor may have taken place in
various ways, and most likely did, according to circumstances, take place in all of them.   In some townships a
chief house might become richer and more prosperous
than the others, until its head possessed a commanding
influence, and the poorer members were glad to become
his dependents.   But the man who had thriven and
become a lord in his own township would be sought as a
protector, sooner or later, by strangers also.   There were
times of warfare between kingdom and kingdom, and
later of Danish harrying and general disorder, in which
old bounds and usages were overridden, and the bonds
of society loosened.   There were times of distress, too,
when freemen were ready to "bow their heads for
meat" to any one who would support them, insomuch
that the neediest of them were driven to become not
merely dependents but bondmen.   Thus the dominion
of the stronger landholders, once set on foot, was increased by the submission of many sorts of people, now
singly, now, perhaps, collectively.   Grants of public

jurisdiction and revenues from the king completed the strength and pre-eminence of the lords ; and this process, repeated all over the country, had long before the Conquest made England into a land of great estates, cultivated partly by personally free dependents and partly by bondmen. But it had not supplanted the smaller free tenancies, of which a great number, chiefly but by no means wholly in the eastern counties, are recorded in Domesday, and the old communal use and tillage of the land wore unaffected in substance by changes of over-lordship and of the legal title and position of the lords.[1]

We may now ask what became of these divisions of land tenure as they existed before the Conquest, and what traces they have left on the modern law ? These traces will appear on examination to be far deeper and more lasting than is commonly known. The inquiry, therefore, is something more than a piece of minute antiquarian curiosity.

First we may dispose of book-land. I have tried to show that its importance as a normal and constant element in the Old-English land system has been over-rated. If this is right, we may the more easily understand the certain fact that we hear next to nothing of book-land after the Conquest. Many of the great estates, probably most, were confiscated on account of the owner's resistance to William. There must have been many cases, however, notably those of religious

[1] See note C in Appendix for a summary, mostly extracted from an address delivered by me as President of the Devonshire Association in 1894, of rival theories on the "village community" question. The controversy is both difficult and interesting, but really makes very little difference to the post-Norman history of the law.

houses, where the substance and enjoyment of possession remained undisturbed. In these cases the form was
none the less superseded by the new Anglo-Norman
theory of tenure and the corresponding forms which it
introduced. The Norman charter, which in strictness
was only evidence of the corporal act of investiture, and
thus returned to the ancient Germanic system, took
the place of the English "book"; and where no real
services were performed by the landholder, nominal
ones were invented to save the credit of the theory.
Religious persons were supposed to hold their lands on
condition of performing divine services [1] which would
assure the spiritual benefit of the grantor and his heirs,
as the lay tenants held theirs by rendering to the lord
the temporal and tangible benefits of military or agricultural aid. And the lands of ecclesiastical corporations
are to this day said to be held by the tenure of *frank-
almoigne or free-alms*, though the explanation which
originally supported the fiction of a tenure has disappeared since the Reformation. [2] Such lands now
represent book-land, so far as anything can represent it
in our modern system. There is no doubt that at least
some of them are in fact ancient book-land which has
been held without a break in title since it was first
granted by some West-Saxon or Mercian king with the
witness and consent of his Witan. [3] Of course no new
book-land was created after the Conquest. ' The Anglo-

[1] Services, that is, not specifically defined or demandable. In
some cases the services were definite, and then the tenure was "by
divine service" strictly so called, in opposition to *frank-almoigne*.

[2] Litt. s. 135, and Coke thereupon.

[3] For example, the manor of Scotter in Lincolnshire. *Archæo-
logia*, xlvi. 371.

Saxon "book" was supplanted by the feudal grant creating a tenure; and of this the written charter was only a common and convenient record, not an essential part.

We have next to consider what became of the folk-land. Whatever remained disposable by the king with the consent of the Witan became the king's land. The king not only dealt with such land without the counsel or consent of the Witan or any one else, but treated it as if it were in all respects his private inheritance. For several centuries no distinction was made between property held and administered by the king in right of the Crown and on behalf of the nation, and property belonging to him as an individual. After the Conquest whatever was found in the king's hands was thrown into one mass with what had come to the Crown by forfeitures and confiscations, and the whole was registered in Domesday as Terra Regis. There is much reason to think, however, that even before the Conquest, from the tenth century onwards, if not earlier, the consent of the Witan, though almost always expressed, was often little more than a formal attestation.

As to folk-land subject to common rights, there is no doubt that much of it went on being occupied and used in the old fashion down to our own time. Indeed historical records about it are scanty, and the modern survival of practices which can be explained only by a general system of common use and enjoyment is the best evidence we have that the system really existed in the past, a circumstance which ought to make us careful in other cases how we draw negative inferences from the dearth of positive evidence in early times. The lands

which in modern times have remained subject to communal customs are variously known as commonable,
open, or intermixed fields, and very frequently as
Lammas lands.   In the last few generations the progress of enclosure and partition has been rapid, and the
amount of these lands has been notably diminished even
within living memory.   It will be convenient, however,
to speak in the present tense of the facts which towards
the middle of this century were put on record by careful
and competent observers as then actually existing.[1]
Another generation earlier more than half the land of
some English counties was under one or another variety
of those usages.   They differ in detail, but the general
type is that from seedtime to harvest the land is
divided among several occupiers, tilling each his own
portion, and after the harvest (that is, on or about old
Lammas day, or the 12th of August in the reformed
calendar, whence the name of Lammas lands) it is thrown
open for pasturage, sometimes to the 'same persons who
have occupied them in severalty, sometimes to a larger
class.   The occupiers for tillage are generally bound to
a customary rotation of crops and fallow, which of itself
is such as to point to days of very primitive farming.[2]
Many commonable hay-fields are also found which are
thrown open earlier in the year, as soon as the hay-

---

[1] Select Committee on Commons Inclosure, 1844. E. Nasse,
Mittelalterliche Feldgemeinschaft, etc. : Bonn, 1869 (Eng. transl. by
Col. Ouvry, published by the Cobden Club, 2nd ed., 1872), where
details are given. The facts collected in Mr. Seebohm's *English
Village Community* also throw much light on these matters.

[2] The regular course is wheat, oats or beans, and fallow. A
four-course rotation is also met with, and exceptionally the bare
alternation of crop and fallow.

harvest is over.   It is significant that these usages are
stated to be most prevalent in those parts of the country
where the soil is most fertile, and the land was therefore taken into cultivation at a very early time.   The
subdivision of the holdings for several cultivation is
extremely minute, so that even a considerable owner of
land of this kind will have it all in little parcels of at
most a couple of acres each, the remnants of the acre-
strips of which a normal holding "lying abroad" in the
common fields was made up throughout the Middle
Ages.[1]   It is found that where this system prevails
the farmers are collected in agricultural villages, whereas
in the parts where complete severalty of ownership is
the rule we find scattered and independent homesteads.
One cannot overlook the historical significance of such
a fact; the conclusion is almost irresistible that the
village in these cases represents an earlier township or
community to which the land belonged.   It is no less
fit to be noted that the country of open and common
fields is also the country of small copyholds; this, how-
over, we shall consider later.

   Another fact of some importance is that, although
in the modern legal theory a parish or township is not
capable of holding lands, yet lands belonging to a parish,
and administered by the churchwardens in aid of its
other sources of revenue, are frequently met with; so
frequently, indeed, that the difficulties of legal title

[1] See Mr. Seebohm's *English Village Community* for details.
The process by which the strips were gradually consolidated may
be seen in various stages in estate maps of the late sixteenth and
early seventeenth centuries, in the possession of the colleges of All
Souls and Corpus Christi at Oxford.   Other public bodies probably
have similar collections, but I have not heard of any so good.

resulting from this state of things were brought to the
attention of Parliament within the present century, and
in one of the Poor Law statutes the churchwardens and
overseers of any parish to which land belongs were
incidentally made a body corporate for the purpose of
dealing with it.[1] Sometimes these parish lands are within
the modern boundaries, but by no means always. For
example, the parish of Sampford Spincy in South Devon
lately held a piece of land in the parish of Tamerton,
as much as twelve miles away. Such outlying lands can
hardly be supposed to have belonged to the township in
ancient times; more probably they represent medieval
gifts to pious uses. It would now be impossible, unless
in specially favourable conditions which may sometimes
exist, to trace the history of these parish properties with
any certainty. In the case I have mentioned nothing
whatever is known about it, all early records of the
parish having been lost by neglect. In some cases the
use of the property for parish purposes is known to go
back to the time of the Reformation or earlier. This,
however, is still consistent with a gift or appropriation
long since the Conquest. But the fact of gifts being
made to the parish at all shows that for the popular
mind it retained its existence as a kind of corporate
body, though the law refused to acknowledge it. And
at last Parliament, as we have just seen, had to bring
the law round again to the popular view.

The village greens which still exist in many parts of
the country may fairly be regarded as a remnant of old
unappropriated common land. Here the modern legal
theory simply reverses the order of the facts. These

[1] 59 Geo. III. c. 12, s. 17 (A.D. 1819).

bits of ground used by the inhabitants for recreation are in most cases ground which never really belonged to any several owner. Not having been appropriated by reclamation or otherwise in early times, and having escaped wholly or in part from the encroachment of the lord or his agents, they remain open for common enjoyment. But the theory of the law-books is that they belonged to the lord, and that in early times he granted rights of enjoyment over it, or allowed them to grow up by way of custom. And though of late years judges have more than once admitted from the bench the historical futility of this theory, it is now hardly possible to break with it altogether for legal purposes. We now speak of a custom for the inhabitants of a parish to dance or to play lawful games at seasonable times on such and such a piece of land, the land being imagined to belong to some person whose ordinary rights over it as owner are limited by the customary use of strangers. This is really fiction and nothing else in the majority of cases; but the fiction is inveterate.

Rights of common have a similar history, though both the facts and the legal treatment of them are more complex. The simpler case of the village green may help us to a clear understanding of the legal nature of a common. According to the doctrine of the books a common is the waste of a manor. It may happen that the wastes of two or more manors adjoin, and sometimes the common, or moor, or whatever it may be called, is a royal forest—that is, a hunting preserve created since the Conquest.[1] The presence of trees, I need hardly

[1] "Foresta regis est tuta ferarum mansio . . . quasi feresta, hoc est ferarum statio."—*Dial. de Scaccario*, i. c. xii.

say, is not required to make a forest in this sense.
The great mark of it is the absence of enclosures.
Dartmoor is a forest, and (but for modern plantations)
trees grow on it only in a few sheltered hollows.
These cases offer peculiarities of their own, which to
the lawyer are extremely curious.   But just now we
will confine ourselves to the more ordinary case of a
common lying wholly within the bounds of a single
manor.   The waste of the manor, then, is in the
modern legal theory so much of the lord's land as his
predecessors have not found it worth while either to
take into cultivation on their own account or to let out
to tenants.   Those predecessors have at some remote
time granted to their tenants various privileges over
this unoccupied land ; the liberty of pasture, or of taking sand and gravel, or cutting underwood, and such
like matters convenient for the use and enjoyment of
their cultivated holdings.   These liberties have ripened
by long continuance into rights which the lord can no
longer withhold.   All the rights of the commoners are
thus conceived as having been carved, as it were, out
of the original full and absolute dominion of some
imaginary predecessor of the existing lord.   It is
allowed, indeed, that in the one case of common of
pasture the tenant's right might be in some measure
independent of the lord's will, being annexed by law to
his tenement if there was nothing to exclude it.   This
is the doctrine of "common appendant."   But the
general theory was as I have stated.   We have great
reason to say again, as we said in the particular case of
the village green, that this theory reverses the facts.
We cannot say it, however, without qualification, for

there is reason to think that in many cases manorial customs which at first sight look like very ancient survivals are the result of arrangements deliberately made in the fourteenth or fifteenth century.[1] But even in those cases, whether they are few or many, the usages were not invented by the tenants or the lord, but were framed, with additions and variations, on customs already established elsewhere. On the whole, then, we may say that rights of common and all similar rights are derived either from the ancient use and enjoyment of undivided common land under the customs of the particular neighbourhood, or from use and enjoyment really granted by lords to their inferior tenants in imitation of the ancient customs. The old common land, then, is represented on the one hand by such remnants of the common system of cultivation as now exist in England, or lately existed ; on the other hand, by rights of common and the like.

Lastly, what became of the folk-land held by individuals as their inheritance, not by the exceptional privilege of a " book " or charter, but according to the varying custom of the country, and without any written evidence of title at all ? It is impossible for us now to get any direct proof about this ; but for my own part I believe that such land went on being held by the old customs for centuries after the Conquest, and is to a great extent represented by copyholds ; a form of tenure which is now fast disappearing, and may be extinct in another generation or two, but on which a large proportion of English land was held down to the

[1] Maitland, "The Survival of Archaic Communities," *Law Quart. Rev.* iv. 36, 211.

present century. We are told in all the books dealing
with the history of our land laws or land tenure, from
Sir Edward Coke downwards, that the copyholder of
the modern and later medieval English system grew
out of the villein of earlier times. The statement is
certainly true in some sense; but it is capable of so
many that it is important to determine which of them
we mean to adopt. The meaning of the proposition
depends on the meaning of its terms. The first of
them is clear enough. We all know, or may easily
know whenever we please, what is meant by a copyholder. A copyholder- is a tenant of a manor who is
said to hold his tenement "at the will of the lord
according to the custom of the manor." This means
that the tenant's rights are nominally dependent on the
will of the lord; but the lord is bound to exercise his
will according to the custom, so that the tenant is
really as safe as if he were an absolute owner. The
lord's petty monarchy over the manor, whatever it may
have been formerly (and there is nothing to show that
it was ever really absolute as regards tenure), is now
strictly constitutional. The tenant's title, however, is
evidenced not by deeds in his own possession, but by
the records of the lord's court, which show the admis-
sion of successive tenants by the lord or his steward.
For this reason the tenant is said to hold "by copy of
court roll." He is generally debarred from some of
the rights of an absolute owner, such as cutting timber
and opening mines, and has to pay fines on alienation;
and often, besides these, the curious and vexatious fine
in kind called a heriot on a succession. These payments represent a price paid for the lord's consent to

admit a purchaser or accept the deceased tenant's heir; which once, no doubt, was arbitrary—in other words, the most the lord could get. In the modern law the money payments have become fixed, but the heriot of the best beast, or sometimes the best chattel of any kind, may still in many cases be demanded. Also there are money rents payable to the lord which once were of substantial value, and often can be made out to have been the full letting value of the land in the thirteenth or fourteenth century. Thus much for a general notion, rough but sufficient for our immediate purpose, of the nature of copyhold tenure.

But as to the other term of the proposition, what do we mean by a villein? As far as the word goes, it is the Latin *villanus*, which in itself means nothing more than an inhabitant of a vill or township. At the time of the Conquest, and long after, the *villanus* was a rustic tenant holding land under a lord, and owing to that lord certain rents and agricultural services. The rents were sometimes in farm produce, but sometimes (and in course of time generally) in money payments representing its commuted average value. The tenure was not reckoned free, but the *villanus* was not necessarily an unfree man; the majority of the rural population were probably unfree as late as the thirteenth century,[1] but how great a majority we cannot say. Nor were these *villani* properly so called even the lowest class of personally free tenants. There were others, described by various names, whose services were more burdensome, and the lowest of these must have been little better off than true bondmen. It is not

---

[1] Pollock and Maitland, *Hist. Eng. Law*, i. 415.

always easy to draw the line between the free and the
unfree tillers of the soil. But there is not the least
doubt that a large number of <u>bondmen</u> existed. The
proper Latin name for a man in this condition was
servus or *nativus.* Probably most of them were descendants of the British population who had been spared
in the English Conquest. At all events, they were
personally in their lords' power, and were at their
mercy in everything short of life and limb. Whatever
they held of land or goods was held only by the lord's
permission and might be recalled at his will. We
know that before the Conquest freemen were not uncommonly driven by want to become bondmen. But
sometimes they stopped short of this degradation, and
accepted land to be held on servile and precarious
terms, but without giving up their personal freedom, or
their rights of property in their movable goods. We
know that similar terms were after the Norman Conquest forced on many Englishmen who had been hostile
to the Normans without actually bearing arms against
them ; and we may suspect that similar arrangements
had centuries before been made, especially in the
western parts, between the conquering Englishman and
the conquered Welshman. There are abundant possible
historical sources of precarious tenures intermediate
between full security and that bare holding on sufferance which hardly ever exists in practice ; and however
troublesome these are to the lawyer when he meets
with them, we really ought to be surprised, if at all,
that there are not more of them. Only the tendency
of usage to become fixed has saved us from a great
deal more trouble of this kind. On the whole, we find,

at and after the time of the Conquest, three distinct types of actual occupiers of the soil.

There are the personally free men, holding more or less land on terms of more or less burdensome service, and called by sundry names accordingly, but on fixed terms in every case. There are the bondmen, who are in a lord's hand and can call nothing their own, whose holdings are precarious, and who are taxed at the lord's will. And there are the degraded freemen (whether the remnant of a conquered race, or decayed members of the ruling one), who are not personally enslaved, but whose holdings are of a servile and precarious kind. Moreover, the holdings retained the character once fixed upon them; so that by successive changes of ownership it might and did happen that the same man would hold some land by free and other by bond service, and the nature of the services did not affect his personal condition. To say that one was a lord's villain was to renounce freedom and all independent rights; to say that one held land of him in villenage was compatible with defending the title in one's own name against a stranger.[1] On the other hand, a bondman might deal as a freeman with any one except his lord, and might, if he could, hold free land, under the risk of the lord reclaiming him. The test of a servile holding was liability to be taxed at the will of the lord. Its other incidents were in practice fixed by usage even at the time of the Conquest, and in many cases the holders acquired some kind of inchoate hereditary right.

If we bear in mind these distinctions, it is not very

---

[1] Year Book, 20 Ed. I. (Rolls ed.), 41.

difficult to form a reasonable conception of the early history of copyholds. Positive proof we can hardly expect, as our authorities are scanty for the first century after Domesday, and we have hardly any detailed records in the shape of court rolls and accounts for another century after that. Unfortunately the whole subject has in modern times been confused by the ambiguous use of words. The meaning of the old *villanus*, which was at first no less honourable a name than our yeoman, became degraded after the Conquest, and both in Latin, and in the French form *villein*, it was used to stand for *nativus*, with which it properly had nothing to do. The old customary tenure by labour-rents was still called villenage, and thus the customary tenants and the bondmen became completely mixed up in the apprehension of modern text-writers.[1] Medieval lawyers, no doubt, strove to be accurate with this awkward nomenclature. When they meant *nativus*, they spoke in express terms of a " villein by blood." They were careful to distinguish the old or privileged villenage, which was really a free though more or less onerous tenure, from the villenage of base and uncertain tenure, and again to distinguish the service due in respect of the land from the personal condition of the holder. But in later times these things were over-looked, and the result was the formerly current account of copyholds: namely, that (in Blackstone's

---

[1] Historical students have gradually worked out the truth piecemeal. Some of our best authorities, however, seem to think that dependent freemen and bondmen were really mixed up by their Norman lords. This, for the reasons given in the Appendix, Note D, seems to me improbable.

language) "copyholders are in truth no other than
villeins, who by a long series of immemorial encroachments on the lord have at last established a customary
right to those estates which before were held absolutely
at the lord's will ":[1] villeins being understood as
villeins by blood or *nativi.* It would be nearer the
truth to say that by a long series of encroachments
and fictions the lords, and lawyers acting in the interest
of the lords, got people to believe that the lord's will
was the origin of those ancient customary rights which
before were absolute.

When we have once shaken off the false theory of
Blackstone (I say of Blackstone, for I cannot find that
anybody stated it so positively before him), the nature
of existing copyhold customs is really enough by itself
to carry conviction of their great antiquity. Of this
kind is the custom of "borough-English," or, as it is
more expressively called in some parts, "cradle-holding,"
by which the course of descent is neither to the eldest
son as at common law, nor to all equally as in the
old tenure of gavelkind which still subsists in Kent,
but to the youngest son exclusively. Such a rule of
descent is very difficult to account for. But the difficulty we now have in understanding it is some proof
that it comes down from a forgotten condition of
society; and the fact that it was so deeply rooted as
to survive the Norman Conquest seems to show that it
was ancient then. Similar customs are found in
various parts of Europe, and in some cases have been
kept up in modern times in spite of the modern law
taking no account of them. Probably the explanation

[1] *Commentaries*, ii. 95.   See Note D.

is that there was a time when each son of a family as
he came of age was entitled to an allotment out of
common land. Thus the sons in turn parted off from
the family and were provided for, and the homestead
was left for the youngest. Such a state of things is
actually recorded in the old Welsh laws. It might be
inferred that the custom as found in England is of
Welsh origin, and is in fact a primitive usage which
has survived not only the Norman but the English
Conquest. In that case, however, we should expect to
find it prevalent not in the south and centre, but in
the west and south-west of England.

Whatever account may be given of particular
customs, we need have no fear in saying that the
modern copyholders are the historical successors of the
Old English landholders who had inheritable titles
according to local custom, evidenced not by writing
but by the witness of the neighbours, and paid dues
and services to a lord. If the copyholders now seem
too few to fill so large a place in the history, we have
to remember that the amount of land held on this
tenure has for a long time been fast diminishing. Late
in the sixteenth century one-third of the land in England was still copyhold. The archaic incidents of the
tenure being found in modern practice inconvenient to
everybody concerned with the land, and productive of
far more vexation to the tenant than advantage to the
lord, the manorial rights have in later times been constantly extinguished by agreement, and of late years
under the powers of requiring enfranchisement on
proper terms given by the Copyhold Acts to both lords
and tenants. In various parts of the country there are

customary estates of the nature of copyhold, but in which the tenant's position is still insecure. He holds for one or more lives, or sometimes for a short term of years; and renewal, though it is the rule, is not a matter of established right. This tenure is common in the western counties, and may fairly be thought to represent the terms on which the conquered Welsh population were allowed by the English settlers to retain their lands. In Cornwall there are or were [1] certain "conventionary tenants" holding by a title renewable at intervals of seven years, the tenant paying a fine on renewal. As the old customs of Brittany present analogies to this tenure not only in substance but in name, it is all but certain that the Cornish custom is older than the English settlement. The same may be said of the peculiar mining customs of Cornwall and parts of Derbyshire, which entitle adventurers to work mines under any man's waste land if he does not work them himself, paying to the owner the customary dues and royalties. In Cornwall this is called "tin-bounding," from the setting out of the working by bounds, which is the adventurer's first step towards establishing his claim. The like custom existed in the mining districts of Devon as long as tin-streaming was there practised.

The detailed pursuit of special and local customs, however—much more the attempt to trace their history and affinities—would lead us too far. Enough has been

---

[1] The conventionary tenements of certain manors of the Duchy of Cornwall were enfranchised by an Act of 1844 (7 & 8 Vict. c. 105). I do not know whether other examples of the tenure remain.

said to show that customs older than the Norman Conquest, and perhaps older than the English Conquest, have been far more persistent, and have left far deeper marks in the modern structure of the law, than was formerly understood. We must pass on to the feudal period of English land tenure, and trace the effects of the feudal doctrines and policy which for so long overlaid the ancient customs without destroying them.

CHAPTER III

THE Norman Conquest was the means of introducing great and systematic changes in the government and laws of England, and not least in the law governing the tenure of land. If we are to fix a date, however, to which to refer the active carrying out of these changes, we must look nearly a century onwards from the Conquest itself. It was the general and uniform jurisdiction of the king's courts, represented by his judges, who regularly went round the country, that achieved the work of breaking up the diversity of local customs and fixing the new pattern of English institutions. This jurisdiction was put into effectual working order under Henry II., and feudalism was at its most perfect stage in England in the first half of the thirteenth century. From the latter part of that century onwards the system underwent a series of grave modifications. Grave as these were, however, the main lines of the feudal theory were always ostensibly preserved. And to this day, though the really characteristic incidents of the feudal tenures have disappeared or left only the faintest of traces, the scheme of our land laws can, as to its form, be described only as a modified feudalism.

In order to do justice to the feudal system we must consider it not only in its proper shape but with regard to its proper and original purpose. From any modern point of view the surviving peculiarities of feudal law, such as primogeniture, can be defended only by those ingenious arguments which, being manifestly begotten of afterthought, appear convincing only to persons who need no conviction. But in the early Middle Ages economical excellence was not the first object of European systems of tenure, and it was impossible to make it so. Before men could settle how to hold and culti-vate their land to the best advantage, they had to deal with the more pressing question how they should make sure of being allowed to hold or cultivate it at all. Feudalism was really a co-operative association for the mutual defence of the members. Considered in its application to the whole of an independent community, it was the military organisation of society appropriate to a time when there were no standing armies, and one able-bodied man needed nothing but arms in his hands to make him as good a soldier as another. A feudal State was a nation ready to take arms. The king or other supreme prince was the commander-in-chief. His immediate feudal tenants were generals, each of whom not only commanded but raised and equipped his contingent. And these contingents again were made up by the contributions of lesser tenants, of whom some were bound to take the field with a certain num-ber of men and horses, some only to serve in person. The plan of every chief and under-chief bringing his own men, who take their orders from him alone, is in itself much older than feudalism. It is pretty well

universal in the early stages of civilisation. We see it
in full force in the Homeric descriptions of the Greek
host before Troy. Marks of it have remained even in
modern military establishments. In the last century a
regiment was regarded as in a manner belonging to its
colonel ; and British regiments were separately recruited
and equipped by their commanding officers almost in
our own time. The peculiarity of the feudal system is
that this type of military organisation has increased
fixity and solidity given to it by making it also territorial.   Land, as the ultimate source of wealth (and at
that time almost the only direct one), is regarded by
the State according to its capacity for supporting the
defence of the nation.   It is not merely bound to con-
tribute to this purpose by way of taxation, as was the
case in England before the Conquest.   Quite apart from
feudalism, the burden of supplying the means of de-
fensive warfare was universal and paramount ; even
in the most favourable grants of public land this was
excepted from the immunities conferred on the holder.
But feudalism does not stop at contribution ; it makes
military service, in many cases personal service, or in
any case definite provision for it, the essence and the
condition of the landholder's title. The land is assigned
to him for the support of his military duties. To some
extent this was the real historical origin of feudal tenures ; in what proportions it combined with other causes
to produce the actual result is outside the business in
hand.[1]   Such is in any case the conception dominating
the system in its finished form.

[1] As to Continental feudalism see Stubbs, Const. Hist. i. 251 ;
and as to the introduction of military tenures in England, ib. 261.

Regarding the feudal tenant as an officer settled on
land rather than as owner of the land, we see the fitness
of the feudal institutions. Both as to the rights and
duties of the tenant, and as to the transmission of them
by descent or otherwise, the efficient performance of the
services is the first consideration. Freedom of alienation is regarded, in our modern way of thinking, as one
of the natural incidents of ownership ; but there was no
place for it in the doctrine of feudal tenancy. The
tenant by military service was no more entitled of his
own motion to put a new-comer in his place than a
soldier on duty to assign his post to another. Feudal
tenants had indeed powers of alienation which ultimately
became equivalent to freedom for all practical purposes :
but these were regarded as in the first instance not
belonging to them as owners, but conferred on them by
delegation from the lord under whose grant they held.
Disposal by will was a thing still more strongly repugnant to the feudal theory. Before the Conquest, as we
have seen, it had been the fashion among the larger
landowners (though perhaps rather as a matter of special
privilege than of common right) ; but the military
tenures put a stop to this. Even inheritance by descent
can scarcely be called an unqualified right in the feudal
system. It existed only when there was mention of
heirs in the original grant of the estate ; and the heir did
not even then succeed as a matter of free and common

In England there was never a complete military feudalism any
more than a complete legal one ; the practice was already inadequate and becoming obsolete before the law was fully defined
(see Pollock and Maitland, *Hist. Eng. Law*, i. 231) ; so that the
military incidents of tenure were soon as useless to the kingdom
as burdensome to the tenant.

right. He owed the lord a payment called relief, which was the price of his full acceptance as the new tenant. In form English law preserves this conception to the present day. Dealing with land as a subject of ownership, like anything else, we should expect a grant of land to a man in unqualified terms to give him the whole interest the grantor was capable of transferring. But land, as it was not so dealt with in the feudal tenures, is still not so dealt with in our legal theory. The grant of land to a man, without specifying what estate he is to take, will to this day give him no interest beyond his own life. In the case of a will the rule has been changed by legislation, and had in various ways been relaxed earlier; but our modern wills of land belong to another and later stage of the history, and must be considered apart. On the principle that a feudal tenancy is not merely a possession, but an office of trust and confidence, it is more difficult to account for inheritance being the rule, or being allowed at all, than for dispositions by will not being allowed. The hereditary character of feudal estates had been established on the Continent, however, long before the feudal period of English law, but still under conditions bearing witness to the difference between the tenure of such estates and complete ownership. Both on the Continent and in England the inheritance of military tenures was governed by a peculiar and appropriate rule of its own, the rule now familiar by the name of primogeniture. On the tenant's death his eldest or only son took the whole of his land, to the exclusion both of daughters and of younger sons.

The actual origin of primogeniture is obscure. More

or less preference is shown to the eldest son in the division of the father's heritage by many customary laws of different nations, European and other. Such a customary law may be found still in force in the Queen's dominions no farther from us than the Channel Islands. On the other hand, we find in many local customs that the same kind of preference is shown to the youngest ; and it is doubtful whether this very general usage of "privileged succession," as Sir Henry Maine calls it, has in truth anything to do with the exceptional rule of exclusive succession. There are traces of primogeniture in the strict sense having existed as a local custom in England apart from feudalism, but to what extent we do not know. Wherever the institution came from, its advantages to both the lord and the tenant in an un-settled state of society, where a man might any day have to keep his goods and land by his own sword, are sufficiently obvious. The same reasons which made against free alienation of that which was not so much property as a post of defence and an office of command were yet stronger against dividing it. We see that where the feudal rules did allow division, as in the case of female co-heirs, an exception was made in the case of a chief place of arms or castle, for the avowed reason of military necessity, *propter ius gladii quod dividi non potest.* Primogeniture, accordingly, grew fast at the expense of other rules of descent. It was imported into England full-grown, and here it obtained, strangely as it appears at first sight, a more complete and lasting success than anywhere else. Its most formidable competitor, the rule of equal division among all the sons (in preference to daughters, not sharing with them as modern ideas of

equal justice would have it), has held its ground only
in Kent. The opposite extreme of the youngest son's
exclusive right is also found as a special and local
custom, sometimes to the confusion of purchasers.
Primogeniture not only drove its rivals into corners,
and became the common law of English landed property, but has outlasted the abolition of the military
tenures to which it was in the first instance confined.
Concurrently with that abolition, however, the power of
testamentary disposition became unlimited ; so that the
rule of intestate descent is now comparatively unim-
portant in its effects.

Primogeniture is only one striking example of the
extension of feudal doctrine and law beyond their original
sphere which took place in England. They assimilated
and superseded, with few exceptions, the customs of the
non-military free tenures ; and even in copyholds the
feudal rules of descent became largely prevalent, with
the help, it may be, of ancient local customs bearing
some resemblance to them. In the presence of the
general law, more widely known and applied than any
particular custom, these customs could not but lose any
distinctive characters they may have had, and become
fused in one body of rules and practice enforced every-
where by the king's courts. It is uncertain how long
the process lasted. In socage land,—the land, that is,
which was held by free tenure, but without military
service,—the contest between primogeniture and gavelkind was still undecided in the thirteenth century.[1] It
was in each case a question of fact whether the inheritance
was divisible by ancient custom. There is reason to

[1] See Note E.

think that the king's judges established a presumption
in favour of primogeniture which in a few generations
became a fixed rule of law. By requiring every one who
claimed a share according to any other custom to prove
strictly that the custom applied to the land in question,
and in default of strict proof applying the feudal rules,
it would not have been difficult to produce in a moderate
time the results that actually came to pass. It must be
remembered that the total number of titles coming within
the jurisdiction of the king's courts was not very large,
a considerable proportion of the land being held on the
inferior customary tenures which, as we saw in the last
chapter, appear in the settled form of the law as copy
holds. The fact that for copyholds, except in parts of
the southern counties where descent to the youngest son
prevails, primogeniture has become the common rule, is
enough to show that in these also some similar process
went on, the manor courts following the fashion set by
the king's judges : but no specific evidence of its course
is now, as far as I know, accessible. Possibly it may
still exist in unexamined court rolls ; but it is extremely
rare to find court rolls earlier than the middle of the
fourteenth century in good or even fair condition.

At the same time that the ancient customs of England were thus feudalised, feudalism itself was modified
or corrupted. Some relaxation of its principles was the
necessary condition of their being so widely applied, and
the system underwent a kind of degeneration in the very
completeness of its victory. The adoption of the feudal
rules as the common law of all English land, but with
the mitigation or omission of their essentially military
features, went side by side with the formation of a

society wherein a strong aristocratic feeling and community of interest prevailed among the larger landowners, and yet there was nothing like the Continental aristocracy of race. These points of contrast between English and Continental feudalism are closely akin, or rather they are two manifestations of the same social and political difference. Where the law recognised no difference of caste, and the king's younger children remained commoners unless and until they were specially called to peerages, it was impossible that the law should make differences between the land of a peer and the land of any other freeholder. Quite in accordance with the general tendency to treat all differences of rank as political rather than personal, it was always considered by English courts that the tenure of land was unaffected by the quality of the person holding it; and this was carried out even in the case of a free man taking land of servile tenure, or a serf becoming a freeholder. The personally free holder of a base tenement performed the services, or got them performed for him, and paid the dues[1] according to the conditions of the tenure. The bondman who acquired a freehold could be challenged on the ground of his personal condition by nobody but his own lord.

Along with this reduction of tenures to a few uniform types, and severance of them from the personal condition of the landholders, there came from the thirteenth century onwards (if not earlier) a general commutation of the services into money payments. This tendency may

---

[1] But it was already disputed in the Middle Ages whether merchet (the fine on a daughter's marriage) could be demanded except from bondmen.

be seen equally in the military obligations of knight-service and in the labour-rents of socage and villein-service. And the feudal tenant's position, from having been a kind of military occupation of the land on special duty, became a complicated form of ownership, subject to periodical and occasional burdens which, having lost their original purpose, appeared as meaningless as they were vexatious.

These "fruits and consequences" of military tenure, as they were called, were of course due to the Crown from its immediate tenants, and were thus a material part of the public revenue. Since the Restoration they have ceased to exist, and are now represented by the excise and the land-tax; but it is impossible to under-stand either the working of the medieval system or its later modification without knowing the nature of these burdens, which by the middle of the seventeenth century had become intolerable, and made the settle-ment of the Restoration a necessity. First there were payments called *aids;* in the theory of our earlier authors they were offered of the tenant's free will, to meet the costs incurred by the lord on particular occasions; but they settled into a fixed custom after-wards, if they had not really done so when those authors wrote. The occasions in question were the ransoming of the lord from captivity; the knighting of his eldest son, "a matter that was formerly attended with great ceremony, pomp, and expense";[1] and the marriage of his eldest daughter. The amounts pay-able for the two latter purposes were assessed at the fixed proportion of a twentieth of the assumed annual

[1] Blackstone.

value of the holding by statutes of the thirteenth and
fourteenth centuries. Then there was the *relief* payable
by an heir of full age on his entry, which likewise
became fixed at an early time. In the case of land
held of the Crown, the king also took a year's profits,
which was called *primer seisin*, and a fine was payable
by the tenant on every alienation of the land. If the
heir was under age, the king or other lord became the
guardian of both the heir and the estate, and rendered
no account of the profits; and on the heir's coming of
age a fine was payable to the guardian for quitting the
land. This privilege of the lord, in many cases a highly
lucrative one, was called *wardship*; and incident to it
was the right of disposing of the ward in marriage,
which appears to have been commonly treated as a
matter of sale and barter in the guardian's interest.
In the case of non-military free tenure a relief of a year's
rent was payable where a rent in money or kind was
reserved, and "primer seisin" if the land was immediately held of the Crown; and the aids for the knighthood of the lord's eldest son or marriage of his eldest
daughter were also due. But the rules of guardianship
were quite different; the guardian in socage was not
the lord, but the nearest of kin to the heir among those
to whom the land could not possibly descend; the
wardship lasted only till the heir was fourteen years
old (when he was free to choose his own guardian until
full age), and, most important of all, the guardian was
accountable. "Such guardian in socage," says Littleton,
"shall not take any issues or profits of such lands or
tenements to his own use, but only to the use and
profit of the heir; and of this he shall render an

account to the heir, when it pleaseth the heir, after he
accomplisheth the age of fourteen years." When the
military tenures and their incidents were finally abolished at the Restoration, this became the general rule ;
by the same statute the father was empowered to
appoint persons of his own choice to be his children's
guardians after his death, if he left them under age.
By an Act of 1886, 49 & 50 Vict. c. 27, the mother, if
she survive, is a guardian, and may also appoint others
to act after her own death. With these additions the
ancient law remains. The statutory power of naming
guardians and the careful provisions of modern settlements have made it almost forgotten.

Thus it appears that in the material point of guardianship the strict feudal doctrines were never applied to
socage lands at all, while the other services and incidents
of feudal tenure rapidly degenerated into a clumsy mode
of taxation in money, or a source of private profit to
the lord of the fee, with great opportunities for corrupt
and oppressive practices.[1] It was no wonder that the
military tenures should be unpopular, or that a variety
of devices should be employed to escape their obligations, which had their effect in suggesting similar
devices for other purposes, and ultimately producing
the complicated and artificial state of our real property
law. The history of our land laws, it cannot be too
often repeated, is a history of legal fictions and evasions,
with which the Legislature vainly endeavoured to keep
pace until their results (and with them the crooked
ways by which they were attained) were perforce

---

[1] The reader may consult Blackstone (*Comm.* ii. 76) for a forcible
and probably accurate sketch of these abuses.

acquiesced in as a settled part of the law itself. We have not yet mentioned an incident common to all feudal tenures, whether military or not—the possibility of the land falling back into the hands of the lord, as representing the original donor, on a failure of the tenant's heirs. *Escheat* (such is the technical name of this event) must have been a sensible branch of the lord's casual profits so long as land could not be disposed of by will. Now that on the one hand alienation by will is allowed without limit, and on the other hand sundry disabilities to take by inheritance are removed, escheat is still possible, but seldom happens. It is yet more seldom, if ever, that it happens in favour of any one but the Crown.

⫽ Feudalism in England tended of itself to settle into a kind of compromise between the rules appropriate to military tenancies, and such as would allow some tolerable convenience of agricultural occupation and peaceful commerce.⫽ But the direct action of the Crown and of Parliament likewise effectually prevented the system from being established in its full consistency. The first decisive step was taken by William the Conqueror when he exacted a direct and universal oath of allegiance to himself, overriding all feudal obligations. That one and paramount sovereignty of the Crown which has ever since been the principle of English executive government, and is stamped in every part on the language and formulas of English law, dates from the Council of Salisbury. From that day, we may truly say in one sense, feudalism was doomed. In another sense we may say that it was preserved by being made harmless against the public order of the kingdom, and

reduced to its fitting place in a polity both coherent
and capable of expansion. What the Conqueror's
wisdom had saved England from was seen later by a
terrible example, when the strength of the king's hand
was for a time paralysed in the evil days of Stephen.
The separation of political allegiance from feudal tenure
cleared the way for the assimilation of the feudal doctrines, as a branch of civil law, by the general custom
and judicial usage of the realm. In the thirteenth century there was a fairly complete system of customary
land laws, as we know by Bracton's exposition. The
feudal services were being reduced to something like
certainty. Primogeniture was not yet fully established
as the common law of non-military free tenancies, but
was rapidly prevailing over the old equal partition
among sons, and other local customs. In other respects
the course of inheritance of freeholds, and the tenant's
power of alienation in his lifetime (by will he could do
nothing with his land, save in some places by special
custom), depended on the terms of the grant. If heirs
were not named at all, the taker had not and could not
give any interest beyond his own life. If heirs were
named, the grant being, for example, to Adam of Stoke
and his heirs, or heirs and assigns, he could alienate
whenever he chose. The interest conferred by a grant
in these terms was and is the largest a subject is capable
of having. It is called an estate in fee simple. "A
man cannot have a more large or greater estate of in
heritance than fee simple."[1] But if a limited kind of

---

[1] Litt. s. 11. The power of alienation was not established all
at once. The history is still obscure in detail, and it seems likely
that for some time the customary law was really vague. "Down

heirs were named, for example, by grant to Ralph of
Hengham and the heirs of his body, or the heirs male
of his body, he could not alienate until some one capable
of succeeding under the special designation was in existence. In the former of the cases just put, Hengham
might alienate as soon as he had a child ; in the latter,
as soon as he had a son. His interest was called in
either case an estate in fee simple conditional, as it fell
short of being a complete fee simple until the condition
of an heir of the named class being in existence was
fulfilled. When it was fulfilled, the special course of
descent prescribed by the original grant was not affected
so long as the tenant retained the land. But if, after
having issue answering the description, he made a grant
in fee simple to another person, say Metingham, then
in Metingham's hands the estate would be a common
estate in fee simple, and descend according to the
general rules of law. Thus if Hengham's lineal descendants, or descendants in the male line, as the case might
be, ceased to exist, this would not enable the lord or
his heirs to claim the estate by escheat.

This wide interpretation of grants limited in their
terms, and intended by the makers to confine the estate
to a particular course of succession, and preserve the
benefit of the grant for the lineal heirs and the chance
of escheat for the lord, was displeasing to the great men
of the kingdom. In 1285 it was declared by Parliament that gifts of this kind should be strictly observed

to the end of the twelfth century the tenant in fee who wished to
alienate had very commonly to seek the consent of his apparent or
presumptive heir." Pollock and Maitland, *Hist. Eng. Law*, ii. 13,
cp. L 310-30.

according to their form, and the tenant should have no power of alienating the inheritance to the prejudice of his issue or of the grantor. This Act is known as the statute *De Donis Conditionalibus*, or in common citation *De Donis*. Under its operation the tenant who would have had a fee simple conditional had only a limited and inalienable estate; and this, as being permanently cut down from the freedom of disposition incident to a fee simple, was no longer called a qualified fee simple, but regarded as a new kind of estate, and called a *fee tail* ("feodum talliatum, taillé"[1]). If after the statute land was granted, say to Metingham and the heirs of his body, then Metingham had all the rights of a tenant in fee simple as to use and enjoyment, but he could not grant away the land for any time beyond his own life. His lineal heirs succeeding under the grant were in the same position. He and they were called tenants in tail, and the land was said to be entailed upon them. Such is the legal and only correct meaning of the term entail, which nowadays is constantly used to express the far more complicated scheme of modern settlements.

Entails, as authorised by the statute *De Donis*, were certainly intended by the Legislature to be perpetual and inviolable. But that intention never took full effect, and before two centuries were over it was wholly set at naught. This is the first of several surprises which the learner of English legal history meets with on his way. He must not expect to find Acts of Parliament in the thirteenth or even the sixteenth

[1] "Jus taliatum, hoc est limitatum, incisum aut restrictum." —Coke, 4 Rep., Pref.

century carried into execution as they are in our own
time. Statutes had to be administered through judges
and lawyers, who were stubborn instruments. They
constantly preferred their own mind to that of the
Parliament, and would contrive and encourage every
means of counterworking a statute they disliked, short
of disobedience to its express terms. We know nothing
of the particular circumstances in which the statute
De Donis was passed. But it is clear that it was
obtained by the great landowners against the feeling of
the country; and that feeling was taken up and made
effectual by the lawyers. Coke, writing long after the
work was done for his time, expressed the tradition of
his order in terms almost of indignation. "When all
estates were fee simple, then were purchasers sure of
their purchases, farmers of their leases, creditors of their
debts; the king and lords had their escheats, forfeitures,
wardships, and other profits of their seigniories; and
for these and other like cases, by the wisdom of the
common law, all estates of inheritance were fee simple;
and what contentions and mischiefs have crept into the
quiet of the law by these fettered inheritances, daily
experience teacheth us." Later still the tradition took
new life in the more polished phrases of Blackstone,
who summed up the mischiefs of inalienable estates, and
testified that by legal authorities they had been "almost
universally considered as the common grievance of the
realm." The methods by which the bonds of the
statute were first relaxed and then slipped off will be
better considered in connection with the other changes
that brought the law of real property to its finished
form. In the meantime we will turn to the other

fundamental statute of Edward I., which is cited as
Quia emptores by its first words, according to the constant
medieval usage still preserved by the Church of Rome,
and to some extent in modern books of Roman law.

This statute was made in 1290. Like the *De Donis*,
it was made in the interest of the great lords; but,
unlike that measure, it was accepted with satisfaction
on all hands. It dealt a heavy blow to the consistency
and elegance of the feudal theory, but made the conditions of land tenure far more simple. It was the
first approximation of feudal tenancy to the modern
conception of full ownership. Before 1290 the feudal
tenant who alienated the whole of his land put the new
tenant in his place as regards the lord; but if he
alienated a part only, the effect was to create a new
and distinct tenure by *subinfeudation*, as it is called.
Thus, if the king granted a manor to Bigod, and Bigod
granted a part of it to Pateshull, Bigod was tenant as
regards the king, and lord as regards Pateshull. Bigod
remained answerable to the king for the services and
dues to be rendered in respect of the whole manor, and
Pateshull to Bigod in respect of the portion Bigod had
granted him. Pateshull, again, might grant over to
Raleigh a portion of what he had from Bigod, and as
to that portion would be Raleigh's lord, and Raleigh
would be his tenant. A person who, being himself a
tenant, is lord of under tenants, is called a mesne lord.
These under-tenures were constantly multiplying, and
not only titles became complicated, but the interests of
the superior lords were gravely affected. The lord's
right to the services of his tenant were in themselves
unchanged by any subinfeudation; but his chance of

getting them practically depended on the punctuality of
the under-tenants, against whom he had no personal
rights, in rendering their contributions to the immediate
tenant.   The profits coming to him by escheat, marriage
of wards, and wardship, were also diminished.   Many
years before the statute in question the great lords had
thought themselves ill-used in this matter.   It was
provided by Magna Charta that no free tenant should
alienate more of his holding than would leave him
enough to perform the services (this shows, by the way,
that at the beginning of the thirteenth century the
feudal services and dues had ceased to represent, if
they ever did represent, anything like the full annual
value of the land).   But this was found inadequate by
the superior lords, and in 1290 the law was funda-
mentally changed.   It was enacted that every freeman [1] might thenceforth dispose at will of his tenement,
or any part thereof, but so that the taker should hold
it from the same chief lord, and by the same services.
The incomer became the direct tenant of the chief lord,
and liable to him, and to him only, for a proportionate
part of the services due in respect of the original holding.   A clause curiously like the introductory clauses
of modern Acts of Parliament confined the application
of the statute to estates in fee simple, and fixed the

[1] Except those holding directly of the Crown, to whom the
same right was extended only in 1 Ed. III. (A.D. 1327).   They
still had either to obtain a licence from the Crown to alienate, or
to pay a "reasonable fine," which in the sixteenth century was
understood to be one year's value of the land, whereas the fee for
a licence was only one-third of the annual value.   The Crown,
therefore, retained a considerable check on its own immediate
tenants.   How it was used I do not know.

day when it should come into operation. Since that day—the feast of St. Andrew in 1290—it has been impossible to create a new feudal tenure of a fee simple estate; and any chief or quit rent now payable to a superior lord out of land held in fee simple must have been created before that time.[1] The statute enabled the fee simple tenant to deal with his land as property, without consulting his lord; and in this respect it was a great economical advance. Probably it was intended to compel the owner of land to be also the occupier, or, at any rate, through his villein and customary tenants, the direct administrator and collector of revenue. If such was the intention, it was before long defeated by the general introduction of leases for years. They were already known in the thirteenth century, but received a great and sudden increase of importance in the fourteenth. The fearful depopulation that followed on the Black Death in 1348 brought about a great scarcity of labour, and made it unprofitable to keep farms in hand; and leases, which till that time had been chiefly used by religious houses as a convenient means of administering their estates, became common everywhere. Leaseholding, however, belongs to what may be called the commercial factor of English land law, and will be considered apart.

---

[1] There is nothing in law to prevent the reservation of rent service or other services on a grant of an estate for life or an estate tail by a tenant in fee simple, but it has never been the practice, except in the case of leases for lives (now going out of use) of the lands of colleges and ecclesiastical corporations. In the State of Pennsylvania the statute of *Quia emptores* has never been received as law, and ground-rents are at this day reserved, when desired, in the form of rent service.

Even a summary view of the mediæval system would be incomplete without some notice of the forms and procedure used in dealing with landed property. Questions of form appear more important, in every system of law which has not reached a highly developed and rational stage, than questions of substance. We may say, if we please, and perhaps it will give a juster notion of the truth of the matter, that questions of substance appear in the disguise of questions of form. This has eminently been the case in the history of English law. Therefore it is never safe for the philosophical lawyer, and still less for the historian, to neglect points of form as being merely technical. An apparently minute technicality may be the veil of a decisive principle. With regard to landed property, the policy of English law as to its disposition has been wrapped up in a series of technical rules, and one may almost say technical accidents. The legalised usage of landowners passed from a simple but cumbrous publicity to an absolute secrecy without any direct assistance from the Legislature, and, in fact, contrary to its intention.

In all early legal systems the transfer of property, or of the more important kinds of property, has to be effected by some kind of public ceremony. Frequently, though not always, the ceremony is of a symbolic nature, and is a substitute for the actual abandonment of possession in favour of another, which is the most obvious way of putting that other in one's place. Possession, it must be remembered, is the first and most important thing in Germanic law, and in the Common Law the Germanic idea, though often obscured in detail and sometimes disregarded by legislation, is

still fundamental. It is hardly too much to say that
even now our law hardly recognises ownership save
under the form of the best or most complete right to
possession. Thus the transfer of land was formerly
completed by the delivery of a turf, a bough, or a
straw taken off the land, the part representing the
whole of the soil itself, or of its produce. There is
much reason to think that in England this was the
manner in which the smaller holders of land, who knew
not the ecclesiastical innovation of written charters or
"books," were accustomed to transfer it before the Conquest. Certain it is that customs of this kind, long
since dwindled to the emptiest formality, still exist in
many copyholds. The transaction was proved by the
witness of the neighbours, who attended for the purpose
of keeping it in memory. When charters were introduced, it would appear that the symbolic delivery was
sometimes also carried out, and recorded in the written
instrument; but in the great majority of Old English
charters nothing of the kind is mentioned. The
"book," in fact (if the view put forward in the
last chapter be correct), was the record, not of an
ordinary conveyance, but of an act of State; and
it was witnessed by officers of State, not by the
neighbours or the popular Court. For a time it
seemed as if the archaic usage of conveyance by actual
or symbolic delivery of possession was to be superseded
by authentic writing. But feudalism came to the rescue
of archaism, and for a time restored it in an even stricter
form. The lord expected to know the dealings of his
tenants with their land: the tenant expected to know if
he was to have a new lord. Alienation of feudal hold-

ings, when it came to be allowed, was subject to the
condition of being notorious. This was assured by
requiring an actual delivery of possession before witnesses and on the land itself—a proceeding accompanied
with different forms in different countries and districts,
and known by the general name of investiture.[1] In
England it was called *livery of seisin*; English practice
required no particular symbolic action or form of words,
provided the intention was clearly expressed, though
some forms are mentioned as usual; and an invitation
to take possession, given in sight of the land, and followed by actual entry in the lifetime of both parties, was
allowed to have the same effect. A charter, or, in later
language, a deed, was generally added, both as a permanent record and for the certain knowledge of the interest
intended to be conveyed. A deed is a writing on parchment or paper, authenticated by the seal of the person
whose mind it purports to declare. Seals were not used
in England before the Conquest, and only by men of
considerable rank for some time after;[2] but before the
thirteenth century the necessity of sealing for a deed
was fully established. Through the Middle Ages every
man of substance had his own particular seal. In our
own time a distinctive seal is hardly ever used, except
by corporations; and the so-called sealing of a deed is
practically nothing but a formal acknowledgment of
one's signature. The process of conveying land by

---

[1] See Ducange, s. v. Investitura. A form of English medieval
feoffment may be seen in the Appendix to the second volume of
Blackstone; the common forms of livery are described, ib. 315.

[2] Cp. Lambarde's *Perambulation of Kent*, s. v. Halling; Palgrave,
English Commonwealth, 2. lxx; Bigelow, *Placita Anglo-nor-
mannica*, 177.

livery of seisin was called a *feoffment;* the deed (a
usual though not necessary part of the transaction)[1]
was first executed, and then livery of seisin was given,
and a memorandum of this was indorsed on the deed,
and usually attested by the same witnesses. As a rule,
the deed was short and simple enough in its language ;
on the other hand, the indispensable livery of seisin
might easily lead to much trouble. For technical
reasons there were cases in which several distinct
liveries were required, as if the land being dealt with
was not all in one county. Then there were the
cases, probably not unfrequent in the Middle Ages,
in which hostile claims or occupation made it
dangerous to enter on the land at all; in such cases
actual entry might be dispensed with. Local notoriety
was pretty well secured by these rules, but at the cost
of much inconvenience, of some bodily risk, and, it may
be supposed, of sundry breaches of the king's peace.
Whether the landowners of those days objected to
publicity for its own sake, as their successors have
persistently done for about three centuries and a half,
does not appear. Legal ingenuity was for a long time,
at all events, directed towards other and more pressing
objects.

A cumbrous and ceremonial publicity was not less
the character of judicial dealings with land. The steps
of procedure in " real actions," as lawsuits concerning a
freehold title were called, were many and slow; moreover
there was another cause of delay, frequently the gravest
of all, in the necessity suitors were under, first of finding

---

[1] Writing was first made necessary by the Statute of Frauds, a
deed only in 1845 (8 & 9 Vict. c. 106).

the king's court, and then of obtaining a hearing. For
the king claimed and exercised exclusive jurisdiction in
all matters touching the freehold, which no doubt was
one chief reason of the decay of the ancient local courts;
the king's justice, before Magna Charta, followed the
king's court wherever he happened to be; and in the
time of which we now speak the king was seldom in
the same place for many days together. Moreover, he
was often in Normandy or elsewhere in his Continental
dominions, so that the suitor might have to cross and
recross the Channel in pursuit of him. Add to the cost
of travelling the heavy fees which had to be paid to the
king's officers to get the cause brought before his court,
and we may be satisfied that in the twelfth and early
thirteenth centuries litigation about landed property
was an even more costly luxury than it is now, or than
it was in the Court of Chancery sixty years ago. This
crying grievance was removed by Magna Charta. The
seat of the king's justice between subject and subject
was fixed at Westminster; and at the same time it was
made accessible in the remotest county by the regular
circuits of the justices of assise. The name of these
justices and of their court is derived from their commission to try the actions for recovering the possession
of land, which were technically called assizes. These
possessory actions were less cumbrous than the "writ
of right" by which the general title to the freehold
was decided; but they were still extremely technical,
and the minute distinctions between the forms appropriate to different circumstances abounded in traps
for unwary pleaders. A tenant of land who thought
himself unjustly deprived of possession was naturally

tempted to fall back on self-help, and re-enter, if he
could, by the strong hand. But he was in danger, if
he did this, of putting himself in the wrong; for there
were several cases in which a wrongful dealing with
land was so far effectual as to deprive the person really
entitled of the summary right of entry which he could
have used against a mere intruder. The true owner who
had lost actual possession and the right of entry was
no better off than a claimant who had never been in
possession; if he wanted to keep the law on his side,
he must resort to the expensive process of a "real
action." Hence it was a great object of the actual
holder of an estate, where his title was questionable, to
go through some of the proceedings which would destroy
any possible right of entry. This, again, was a matter of
trouble and expense, but it often gave practical security.
Further details would not be to our purpose; but this
much it is worth while to bear in mind, as helping
to explain why titles to land were constantly doubtful
in the medieval period of English law, and how such a
state of things was found tolerable enough in practice
to escape organic reform. It must also be remembered
that the shifts and fictions which appeared to our fathers
of the Reform Bill time roundabout, cumbrous, absurd,
and barely honest, were introduced as a deliverance from
things yet worse. The old-fashioned action of ejectment,
with its dummy plaintiff appearing as the lessee of the
real plaintiff, and the dummy "casual ejector," who
wrote to the real defendant as "your loving friend," was
more grotesque but less inconvenient than an assize of
novel disseisin.

It will be gathered from what has been already said

that the mediæval land system of England, such as
we find it in Bracton's exposition, never really existed as
a perfect system.   We have seen that legislation broke
in upon it almost before it was completed.   We have
next to see how the growth of three centuries more produced a fabric substantially identical with the law which
men still living remember as their practical study, and
how that growth, driven into perverse courses, was such
as to make the total result, to use Macaulay's term for
one portion of it, a barbarous puzzle.

CHAPTER IV

LEGISLATION AND TRANSFORMATION

FEUDALISM as applied to land tenure in England carried with it almost from the first the seeds of its own destruction. Between the reigns of Edward I. and Henry VIII. they took root and brought forth such fruit as led to a gradual but complete transformation. First let us watch the fortunes of the law of entail.

"Infinite were the scruples, suits, and inconveniences," says Coke,[1] "that the statute of 13 Ed. I. De Donis Conditionalibus did introduce, which intended to give every man power to create a new-found estate in tail, and to establish a perpetuity of his lands, so as the same should not be aliened nor letten, but only during the life of the tenant in tail, against a fundamental rule of the common law, that all estates of inheritance were fee simple." The fetters of the "new-found estate in tail" were grievous to all sorts of people except the great landowners, and various attempts, it appears, were made in Parliament to procure the repeal of the statute. But the landowners were strong enough to hold what they had won against any direct attack; and legal ingenuity set to work to turn the position which it was impractic-

[1] Pref. to Rep. Part 4, cf. 6 Rep. 40.

able to storm. This was partly effected within a short
time by the application of doctrines which now seem to
us of the most technical and arbitrary kind, and yet in
their origin were intended to fulfil, and did fulfil well
enough, the purpose of giving security to purchasers,
and lessening the danger of stale or fictitious claims of
title. They were devised for the case of tenants in fee
simple, and before the statute *De Donis* was thought of;
but the judges treated them as applicable to acts of a
tenant in tail, except so far as their application would
have obviously reduced the statute to a nullity. The
holders of an estate tail were not regarded, as they
might have been, and as the holders of settled estates
are still in those Continental countries where settlements
exist, as a series of mere life-tenants, of whom each
comes into his predecessor's place by way of "substitu-
tion." The grantee of the new limited estate still had
an estate of inheritance which might continue for ever;
he was "chief owner of the land," subject to the statutory
deprivation of power to dispose of it to the prejudice of
his issue, or, in default of issue, the persons (if any)
designated in the grant to take in remainder,[1] successively
or otherwise, and ultimately the donor and his heirs.
Having the freehold, the tenant could lawfully deal with

---

[1] When a tenant in fee simple grants a limited estate, such as
an estate for life or in tail, the residual interest not thus disposed
of is itself an estate capable of being separately dealt with. If, by
the same conveyance, the grantor parts with it, it is called a
remainder; if he keeps it, it is called a reversion. The process of
subdivision may be indefinitely repeated, the fee simple being
regarded as a kind of fixed quantity out of which any number
of "particular estates" may be "carved": the sum of them all
makes up the fee simple, as the bits of a Chinese puzzle make up
the square.

it in his lifetime; if he professed to deal with the fee simple, that was only an excess of authority, not a wholly unauthorised act; and the effect of a feoffment by him (the solemn and accustomed assurance mentioned at the end of the last chapter) was to work a *discontinuance;* that is, his issue had after his death no right to enter on the land and turn out the intruder, but had to resort to the expensive course of asserting their title by process of law, or, in the technical phrase, they were "put to their action." If the alienation was accompanied by a *warranty*—that is, a covenant by the grantor that he and his heirs would warrant the title and enjoyment of the land to the grantee and his heirs—there ensued the further consequence that the very person who claimed to set aside his ancestor's alienation as unauthorised might—under certain conditions, which it is needless, and hardly possible, to specify here—find himself bound by the warranty to defend it, and in case of eviction to compensate the tenant by providing him with lands of equal value.[1] Practically, therefore, it was often possible for the actual possessor of land to give to a purchaser a better title than he had himself. And by such means there is much reason to think that the operation of the statute *De Donis* was to a considerable extent cut short from the very first.

It was not till the fifteenth century, however, that a completely effectual method of breaking through the statutory restraint on alienation—or "barring the entail" as we say—was in regular use. This was an elaborate

[1] The learned reader may see more in Butler's notes to Co. Litt. 191a (vi. 8), 327, and 373b, which deal fully with this intricate subject.

form of collusive lawsuit called a recovery—first a feigned or fictitious recovery—afterwards, when it was well established and familiar, a " common recovery "—and depending for its efficacy on the doctrine of warranty just mentioned. The device, in its simplest form, was of this nature : the tenant in tail (let us call him Littleton) being in possession, some person (say Brian) acting in concert with him would bring the real action, called a "writ of right," for the recovery of the freehold (whence the name of the proceeding), claiming to be himself the true owner. Littleton, instead of defending his title for himself, would "vouch to warranty" a third person (say Catesby), from whom or whose ancestors he professed that his title was derived, and who was supposed bound to warrant the tenant against all comers. Catesby, the " vouchee," as he was called, was brought in as a party, and acknowledged the warranty. Brian, the nominal plaintiff, then asked and obtained leave of the Court to " imparl," or privately confer with him, thus providing —if one may be so irreverent as to take an illustration from the stage—a sort of carpenter's scene to cover the production of the final effect. When Brian came back into Court as if to report the result of the " imparlance," it was found that Catesby had disappeared, "departed in contempt of the Court," as it was formally recorded. Thereupon judgment went by default against Catesby, and the lands were awarded to Brian for an estate in fee simple ; as to Littleton, he and his heirs in tail became entitled to a recompense in lands of equal value against Catesby, by virtue of his supposed warranty. Thus, if Littleton's lineal heirs, who would otherwise have succeeded to the entailed estate, were to make any claim on

it in the future, the answer to them would be that their
only remedy was against Catesby, through whose default
a stranger claiming in some wholly independent right,
or in the technical phrase "by title paramount," had
deprived them of their inheritance. It remained to deal
with the land according to the preconcerted arrangement : this was the affair not of the Court but of the
parties. If Littleton's purpose was to make a sale to
Brian, then Brian had only to keep the land in which the
judgment of the Court gave him full title and possession.
If not, Brian would dispose of it according to Littleton's
directions, by reconveying it to Littleton for an estate
in fee simple, or otherwise as might be desired.

The proceeding is here stated, as above said, in its
simplest form ; and it is supposed that all the steps in
the collusive action are really taken in the regular way.
But the practice of later times, as described by Blackstone, and minutely explained by the text-writers on the
law of real property before 1833, was more artificial and
complex. The action was not merely collusive, but
fictitious. Nothing was really done in the Court of
Common Pleas or its offices, after the issue of the writ
which commenced the supposed proceedings, but the
making up of a record stating, as in the case of a genuine
action, the demand, defence, voucher, imparlance, default,
and judgment ; the same or equivalent fees, however,
were paid to the officers of the Court as if everything
had been done in detail. Only where the party "suffering the recovery" was a nobleman, he did appear in
Court, and a serjeant went through the form of pleading
for him, as I learn on the authority of those who
remember the old practice. On the other hand, the

form was complicated by additional precautions intended to make sure that every possible claim of the inheritable issue of the tenant in tail, or of those who in their failure would become entitled under the further dispositions of the grant in tail, or ultimately of the original grantor and his heirs, should be effectually barred.   The developed modern shape of a "common recovery" can hardly be understood by any one but a special historical student of the law, nor is there any need that it should. It was possible, even after these developments, to raise doubts whether the fiction was in theory quite satisfying; and the rationalising lawyers of the eighteenth century, while some of them at least inclined to think these doubts unanswerable, dismissed them as idle, and considered recoveries "as common assurances, and not at all as real transactions," the artificial reasoning by which a systematic justification of them was attempted being "a thing in its nature inexplicable."[1]   One question, however, may naturally occur to the candid reader, and must not be neglected.   Was not the vouchee, Catesby, as we called him in our imaginary example, put in an extremely awkward position by being made liable to find a recompense in value for the tenant in tail's issue?   And how was he induced to take such a risk?   No doubt the position would have been anxious and dangerous for a man of substance: for, in the Middle Ages at any rate, the Court could not have confessed that it had lent the forms of its most solemn proceedings to a concerted evasion of the statute.   But all trouble on this score was avoided by

[1] Willes's Reports, p. 449; cf. Blackstone, ii. 360. This view is in substance much older; cf. Coke, 5 Rep. 40b, 10 Rep. 42a.

choosing as vouchee some one who notoriously had no
lands to make recompense withal, and therefore was, as
we now say, not worth powder and shot. In later
times this office was assigned by settled usage to the
crier of the Court, who in this capacity was called "the
common vouchee," and thus cheerfully and, we presume,
not ungainfully passed his life, or so much thereof as
was covered by the legal terms, in perpetual contempt
of the Court of Common Pleas and liability to be fined
at the king's discretion.[1] It may also seem that the
nominal plaintiff in the action must have been greatly
trusted by the parties: for what if after the judgment
in his favour he disavowed the arrangement, and insisted on taking the thing seriously and remaining in
possession? He had the strongest possible title on the
face of the proceedings, and no remedy known to the
old common law could touch him. It is possible that
in the earlier days of common recoveries everything
was really left to his honour. But before the latter
end of the fifteenth century the growing jurisdiction
of the Chancellor, of which we shall have to speak
presently, had ample means of enforcing the fulfilment
of his undertaking according to its intention. In later
times the ingenuity of conveyancers made assurance
doubly sure by a complication of provisoes and counter-
checks, which it is needless to specify.[2]

---

[1] It appears that one Jacob Morland held this curious position
in Blackstone's time ; see the form in the Appendix to vol. ii. of
the *Commentaries*. The common vouchee or his deputy got four-
pence for each recovery. (Appendix to 1st Report of R.P. Commissioners.)

[2] *Cf.* Blackstone, ii. 363, and Appendix. The practice of the
early nineteenth century was even more elaborate.

There was another and more ancient proceeding
called a fine, differing from a recovery in that the
collusive or friendly action was not pursued to judgment, but compromised; the name is from the "final
agreement," *finalis concordia*, which was the last step,
"quia imponit finem litibus." Fines could be used to
some extent for the same purposes as recoveries, and
were favoured by statutes which in various ways increased their efficacy; but their action was not so
certain or complete. On the other hand, they were
the proper and sufficient mode of assurance in some
cases where a recovery was unnecessary or inapplicable.
In modern practice their regular use was in dealing
with the lands of married women, which could not
otherwise be effectually conveyed either by the wife or
by the husband. It does not seem needful to say anything more of them here.

The method of barring entails by means of recoveries
is commonly dated, as a settled practice, from the year
1472. A reported case of that date is said to mark
the time when the convenient though cumbrous fiction
obtained full judicial allowance. It appears to me
(though indeed it is of no consequence) that this report, standing alone, would hardly bear out the common
inference, and that our real authority is a statement
made by Coke, which only professes to give the date
approximately.[1] This, however, we may be content to

[1] Reeves, *Hist. Eng. Law*, iii. 323; 6 Co. Rep. 40a. The earliest
express reference to Taltarum's case (the name was really Talkarum,
see Mr. F. W. Maitland's note in *Law Quart. Rev.* ix. 1) I have met
with is in the arguments in Mary Portington's case, 10 Rep. 37a. Coke
himself evidently thought the doctrine and practice were older, *ib.*
37b, 38a. I suspect the extreme oddity of the name has some-

accept; and there is no doubt about the main fact,
which is, that from the latter part of the fifteenth
century onwards (if not earlier) a tenant in tail might
safely use the form of a common recovery to make
himself, or any purchaser from him, a tenant in fee
simple. The modern scheme of strict settlements dates
only from the Restoration; and the intervening space
of about two centuries has therefore been aptly called
a period of comparative freedom of alienation. When
this freedom of the tenant in tail was once established,
the judges made short work of all attempts to encumber
it with any freshly devised restrictions. Ingenious
founders of estates endeavoured from time to time to
impose on their descendants conditions or provisions
against alienation which might restore in their particular
cases the full effect of the statute *De Donis;* but it was
invariably held that such dispositions were repugnant
to the nature of an estate tail, and that the tenant
could not by any means whatever be restrained from
"suffering a recovery," and thereby acquiring or conferring a fee simple. The process of a recovery was
treated with a kind of mystery and special reverence,
and Coke tells us how one Hoord, in a case before the
House of Lords, "rashly and with great ill-will in-
veighed against common recoveries, not knowing the
reason and foundation of them; who was with great
gravity and some sharpness reproved by Sir James

thing to do with the acceptance of Taltarum's case as an historical
landmark. The real point was not to establish the validity of the
proceedings in the recovery itself, but to determine that the issue
in tail must be content with their imaginary recompense in value
against the ultimate vouchee, and (what was more) that those in
remainder were also fully barred.

Dyer, then Chief Justice of the Common Pleas, who said he was not worthy to be of the profession of the law who durst speak against common recoveries, which were the sinews of assurances of inheritances, and founded upon great reason and authority ; *et non sunt capti hoc verbum.*[1]   It may be as well to add that the same doctrines and inventions which served to break the strength of the statute *De Donis* were in themselves capable of being used in various other cases as instruments of downright fraud, and were prevented from being so used only by a series of special enactments, which, together with their causes, are now all but forgotten.

Recoveries had originally served another purpose: their first invention was due to the ingenuity of the clergy.   Religious houses abounded in England, and much of the best land of the kingdom was in their hands by virtue of ancient grants made by pious kings and under-kings, and of additional endowments received from kings and great men since the Conquest.   The monasteries were, except one or two municipal corporations, the only power in the land capable of representing the arts of peace with such weight of wealth and ability as to make head against the military lords. Early medieval chronicles show the abbots as stout, and often successful, litigants in the maintenance of their rights and privileges.   The Crown and the secular lords very soon became jealous of them for political and, still more, for financial reasons.   We have seen that a material part of the revenues of the Crown was derived from the payments made by feudal tenants on succession

[1] 10 Rep. 40a.

and other events. Now the religious communities were exempt from these payments in two ways. The lands they enjoyed by original grants creating a fresh tenure (or, in the construction put on them by lawyers after the Conquest, deemed so to do)[1] were not held on feudal conditions at all: the only service the monks had to render to the donor was to pray for his soul and the souls of his kindred, a purpose associated with religious foundations, in one shape or another, from the Atlantic to the Indian Ocean.[2] If land held in fee simple by military tenure were granted over to a religious house, it escaped the feudal burdens by reason of the new tenant being a corporation. For the very meaning of a corporation is that a changing series of successive persons (whether being many at one time, as the mayor, aldermen, and burgesses of a town, or the master, fellows, and scholars of a college, or an abbot and his convent, or but one at a time, as a bishop or parson) is treated by the law as one continuing person. This artificial person cannot die, or be in guardianship as an infant, or perform military services. Thus when land was held by a corporation (and religious corporations were the most important class before the monasteries were dis-

---

[1] See pp. 35, 36 above.

[2] "And they which hold in frankalmoigne are bound of right before God" (this means that they might be compelled by the ecclesiastical courts) "to make orisons, prayers, masses, and other divine services, for the souls of their grantor or feoffor, and for the souls of their heirs which are dead, and for the prosperity and good life and good health of their heirs which are alive. And therefore they shall do no fealty to their lord, because that this divine service is better for them before God than any doing of fealty."—Litt. s. 135. No new tenure of frankalmoigne could be created, except by the Crown, after the statute of *Quia emptores; ib.* s. 140.

solved) the king or other chief lord lost what were called
the fruits of the tenure in any case. Naturally the
secular lords were not disposed to let this process continue unchecked: and some years before the statute *De
Donis* an Act of Parliament, reinforcing a somewhat
vague provision in Magna Charta, prohibited the acquisition of lands by religious or other persons, "whereby
such lands or tenements may any wise come into mortmain." The reasons given in the preamble are the loss
of services "which at the beginning were provided for
defence of the realm," and of escheats to the lords; if
the reader likes, he may believe that Edward I. and
his advisers were also alive to the social disadvantages
that would ensue from the unlimited withdrawal of land
from commerce. But the economic changes which made
land really an article of commerce began only in the
period of depopulation and great enclosures, from a
century and a half to two centuries later. However,
the religious houses did not sit down under this prohibition. Indeed attempts were made to procure the
repeal of the statute;[1] but in the meantime, the clergy
and their willing benefactors set about compassing their
end by collusive actions, in which the benefactor—now
unable to make a direct gift to the abbey or other
ecclesiastical society—was sued by it on a pretended
claim of title, and let judgment go by default. In the
same session of Parliament with the statute *De Donis*
order was taken against this device; but, having once
become familiar to legal minds, it survived, as we have
seen, in a new and wider application. For the rest, the
Statute of Mortmain of Edward I., though recast in a

[1] Stubbs, ii. 126.

modern form,[1] is still substantially in force.[2]   No corporation, ecclesiastical or civil, can hold land in England, save under a grant made before the statute, or a licence from the Crown, or the authority of some Act of Parliament.   The word *mortmain* is a transcription rather than translation of the Latin *manus mortua*, a term probably used, as Mr. Digby suggests, because the regular clergy against whose endowment this legislation was chiefly directed were treated for legal purposes as dead, "civiliter mortui."   Coke's explanation [3] (after mentioning two or three wild ones "framed out of wit and invention") is that "the lands were said to come to dead hands as to their lords, for that by alienation in mortmaine they lost wholly their escheats, and in effect their knights-services for the defence of the realme, wards, marriages, reliefes, and the like; and therefore [it] was called a dead hand, for that a dead hand yeeldeth no service."   Whatever be its exact derivation, the expression was felt to be forcible and appropriate, and has passed into common speech.   Of late years it has been inexactly made use of in reference to family settlements, as if the "dead hand" were the hand of the settlor by whose grant the successive interests are limited, to use a technical but in this connection an easily understood word.

The difficulties thrown in the way of ecclesiastical persons and bodies acquiring land are connected with the rise and growth of a doctrine which (together with the undesigned effects of legislation intended to cut it

[1] By the Mortmain and Charitable Uses Act, 1888.   An amending Act of 1892 facilitates gifts to local authorities for purposes within their statutory powers of acquiring land.

[2] On the connection of this with *Quia emptores* as part of a general policy, see Stubbs, ii. 113, 122.   [3] Co. Litt. 2b.

short) has profoundly modified our land laws, impressing
on them a great deal of their peculiar modern form, and
fostering, if not creating, the luxuriant intricacy which
makes them the despair of the unlearned. I mean the
doctrine of Uses, with its offshoot, the law of Trusts.
Briefly, the main lines of the story are these. Disabilities to hold land as the recognised feudal tenant,
or the fear of civil troubles and forfeitures for treason
thereupon ensuing, or the desire of escaping feudal
burdens, or making beneficial dispositions of a kind
not sanctioned by the common law, induced men to
screen the real use and enjoyment of landed property
behind the names and presence of titular owners, of
whom alone the ordinary judicial authority could take
notice. These persons, duly constituted as legal tenants,
were a shield to the beneficial owner against a variety
of accidents, of which the mere possibility might then
be a potent enough cause of disquiet. As between
himself and the legal holder, the beneficial holder's
claim to have the substantial enjoyment was at first
merely precarious. In course of time it was protected
by the supreme power of the king, exercised not by his
ordinary courts, but through his Chancellor as dispenser
of an extraordinary and overriding justice. Then
came jealousies on the part of the Crown and the great
lords ; again their privileges and revenues were in
danger of being undermined by subtle evasions. An
attempt was made to reverse the process by one bold
legislative stroke. The Statute of Uses attempted to
reunite the nominal and the substantial ownership which
the practice of cunning men had separated. But the
legislative had once more reckoned without the judicial

power. There was no more willingness than there had been in the case of the statute *De Donis* to carry out the intention of Parliament. Not only, as in that case, was the intention evaded, but by means of a super-subtle interpretation the Statute of Uses was made the instrument of its own discomfiture; it became a land-mark and a fresh starting-point in the development of the system it was intended to destroy. The points thus indicated shall be now set forth with the least possible technicality; to hold out the promise of none would be an idle and impracticable profession.

"From a very early period the bishops and heads of religious houses, as one contrivance for evading the laws prohibiting alienations in mortmain, procured lands to be conveyed in fee simple to some friendly hand, upon trust that they and their successors should be permitted to enjoy the profits."[1] This contrivance, like others, was cut short by Parliament, and effectually as regards its original purpose;[2] but, as in the case of recoveries, it was quickly taken up by laymen who perceived the extent and usefulness of its application. In such a conveyance the land was said to be granted to the intermediary person or persons (there were generally several of them) *to the use* of the beneficial owner, and these persons, taking as they did the legal title, by the regular ceremony of feoffment (explained above, pp. 75, 76), were said to be enfeoffed, or to be feoffees, to uses. As to the beneficial owner, he was described by the uncouth phrase, *cestui que use*, he for

---

[1] Spence, *Equitable Jurisdiction of the Court of Chancery*, i. 440.

[2] 15 Rich. II. c. 5 (A.D. 1391).

whose sake the use is: no single word was ever found
to take the place of this, and at the present day
English lawyers have to speak of *cestui que trust*.[1] Such
were the terms most commonly employed; but the
word *use* was not (as for creating estates at common
law certain appropriate words were) a matter of
necessity. "Trust" or "confidence" would serve as
well, or indeed anything clearly showing the intention.
Assuming the feoffees to uses to be willing and faithful
instruments of the beneficial owner, his advantages
were great. Though he were involved in the civil
strife of York and Lancaster, and dealt with as a
traitor by victorious enemies, the land would be secured
for his children; for it legally belonged not to him but
to the feoffees to uses, and therefore was not forfeited
by his attainder. For the same reason nothing was
payable to the over-lord on his death; there could be no
legal succession while any of the feoffees remained alive,
and herein was the convenience of naming several in
the first instance. The numbers might be kept up
from time to time by new conveyances, as is the
common practice to this day with bodies of trustees
established for charitable and public purposes. Again,
there was by law no power to give lands by will
(except in some cities and towns by special custom);
but the possessor of lands in use could without any
formality at all give directions to the feoffees in his
lifetime, or by testamentary declaration as to the

---

[1] In the case of an estate for the term of a life or lives other
than the tenant's (as a lease for lives), the person whose life is
named is called the *cestui que vie*. I know no other example of
this construction.

enjoyment of them after his death.[1] In this case the feoffees were said to hold the lands to the uses of his will. It was also possible to employ the method of conveyance to uses, and it was not unfrequently employed for the less laudable purpose of evading creditors. The debtor made over his lands to some friend on the understanding that he should still have the profits, and betook himself to one of the many sanctuaries or liberties where personal process could not be executed against him. "There were two inventors of uses, fear and fraud," said Coke in a summary phrase; Bacon adds, and rightly, the desire of larger powers of disposition than were known to the common law ; but fraud would, in Coke's eyes, perhaps include that as well.

Down to the end of the fourteenth century or later the interests of the possessor in use were protected only by the honour of the feoffees, though he could ensure a certain measure of safety by being one of them himself, which was a very common practice. The ecclesiastical courts dared not interpose in a matter of conscience which so nearly concerned the title to land ; the king's ordinary courts could not recognise interests which those who created them had studiously put outside the scope of the common law, for the very purpose of avoiding the risks and burdens of legal ownership. So completely was an *use* of lands ignored that if the feoffee chose to treat the "*cestui que use*" as a mere trespasser, there was no legal defence to his action. Such a state

---

[1] Many examples of such declarations may be seen in *The Fifty Earliest English Wills in the Court of Probate, London*, edited by Mr. Furnivall for the Early English Text Society.

of things could not go on indefinitely; the quantity of land held by feoffees to uses increased year by year till it comprised the greater part of the realm, and the uncertainty of titles depending on mere private understanding became intolerable. The judges might in more than one conceivable way have given some indirect protection to the beneficiary;[1] but recourse was had to the extraordinary jurisdiction of the Chancellor, a power still fresh, flexible, and ambitious. It was then held that the king was in a real sense the fountain of justice. His justice was not exhausted by the functions of the regular tribunals which guided it, so to speak, in the channels of its common application. There remained a supreme executive discretion which might be used on special occasions, a discretion which (according to modern doctrine at least) could not directly abrogate the common law, but might supply its defects or temper its application. This discretion was exercised through the Chancellor, and was the foundation of the whole system of the Court of Chancery; the isolated petitions by which aggrieved subjects begged for its exercise were gradually moulded into regular pleadings, and the transcendent action of the king in his attribute of justice became the settled process of the Court. Thus the possessor of land in use complaining of want of faith on the part of the feoffees, would beseech the Chancellor to relieve him "for the love of God, and in the way of charity." The king's charity, when the Chancellor decided to exercise it, was masterful. Although the feoffee in trust could not be disturbed in his legal title and possession, yet, if he refused to dispose of the

[1] Note F.

enjoyment and profits in the manner that seemed to
the Chancellor agreeable to good faith and conscience,
he might be sent to prison for contempt of the king.
Once habitually put in use, this power became by rapid
steps a normal and systematic jurisdiction. The use
of lands, as distinguished from the apparent feudal
tenancy or "legal estate," became hardly less secure
and a more convenient form of ownership. Broadly
speaking, it resembled legal ownership in everything
but the burdensome incidents; and not only the original
feoffees were bound by the confidence of their grantor,
but so were persons taking the legal estate from them
by purchase with knowledge of their fiduciary office,
or by succession or other gratuitous title in any case.[1]
In other words, the Chancellors extended the conscien-
tious obligation on which their jurisdiction was founded
from the actual feoffee to uses to every one claiming
title through him who had not honestly given value
for the land in ignorance that his vendor was committing a breach of faith. As Bacon said, "The Chancery
looketh further than the common law, namely, to the
corrupt conscience of him that will deal with the land
knowing it in equity to be another's." These principles, though shifted in their application by the means
and in the manner to be forthwith described, are not

---

[1] I have thought it convenient, as the learned reader will see,
to use "purchase" in the text in its popular sense. The man of
business (if I have such a reader) may be helped by the analogy of
the special rights and immunities allowed to the *bona fide* holder
of a negotiable instrument; the technical principles in the two
branches of law are different, but the policy is the same. An ex-
cellent summary of the law of Uses before the statute may be seen
in Blackstone, ii. 330, 331.

obsolete; the working out of them has produced the whole structure of that part of the modern law of the Court of Chancery, technically called Equity, which regulates the vast amount of property, movable and immovable, held in trust throughout England. Thus the beneficial titles to a large proportion of the land in the kingdom were being drawn into the exclusive jurisdiction of the Chancellor.

Notwithstanding the difficulty and expense that must have attended an application to the Chancery as compared with proceedings at the assizes, this jurisdiction was apparently popular. But the Crown and the great lords once more took alarm. In the fourteenth and fifteenth centuries a series of statutes made the " *cestui que use* " subject to certain liabilities, as if he were legal owner of the estates, and in one or two points gave him corresponding powers, but more for the benefit and security of purchasers than for his own.[1] At last, in 1535, the Parliament of Henry VIII. passed "an Act concerning uses and wills," which has ever since been known as the Statute of Uses, and is one of the fundamental and peculiar points of our modern law of real property. The intention was to abolish the system of uses altogether, and reunite the beneficial enjoyment of land to the legal estate; it was likewise intended to abolish the power of disposing of lands by will, which had been introduced by the machinery of uses, and was now in common exercise.[2]

[1] Blackstone, ii. 332.

[2] Our chief authorities for the intention of the Statute of Uses are the preamble of the statute itself, and the generally similar statements made by Coke in his report of Chudleigh's case (1 Rep. 113a), and

The statute[1] declared that "by the common laws of
this realm lands, tenements, and hereditaments be not
devisable by testament, nor ought to be transferred from
one to another but by solemn livery and seisin" (feoffment), "matter of record" (judicial process entered on
the records of the court, that is, fine or recovery),
"writing sufficient made *bona fide* without covin or
fraud" (this clause lacks construction, but is, I think,
to be understood as explaining or summing up the two
previous heads, unless possibly it means leases for years) ;
nevertheless, the preamble proceeds, "divers and sundry
imaginations, subtil inventions, and practices have been
used, whereby the hereditaments of this realm have
been conveyed from one to another by fraudulent feoffments, fines, recoveries, and other assurances craftily
made to secret uses, intents, and trusts," and also by
wills, formal or informal, "for the most part made by
such persons as be visited with sickness, in their extreme
agonies and pains, or at such time as they have scantly

Bacon in his unfinished Reading on the Statute. I do not find it
easy to make out in detail what either of these authors really means
by the restoration of the common law which is supposed to have
been the object. Bacon seems to take a more benignant view of
Uses than Coke, who would have liked to treat the whole system
as a nuisance to be rigorously abated. Without attempting to
fathom all the learning of Chudleigh's case, one may pretty safely
say that Coke would have looked with unmixed disgust on such
inventions as the "name and arms clause" of a modern settlement ; and it is probable that such, among other things, were the
dispositions which the statute was intended to frustrate.

[1] *Revised Statutes*, vol. i. p. 452. I have modernised the spelling, which throughout the statutes of Henry VIII. is in a stage
of confused transition. Its "dyverse and sundry ymaginacions,
subtile invencions, and practises" are amusing, but would distract
a reader not familiar with the matter.

had any good memory or remembrance"; all which
tended to the loss of feudal dues, services, and forfeitures, to uncertainty of title such that "scantly any
person can be certainly assured of any lands by them
purchased, nor knowen surely against whom they shall
use their actions or executions for their rights, titles,
and duties," and moreover to "manifest perjuries by
trial of such secret wills and uses," and finally to "the
utter subversion of the ancient common laws of this
realm." And therefore, "for the extirping and extin-
guishing of all such subtil practised feoffments, fines,
recoveries,[1] abuses, and errors heretofore used and accustomed in this realm," it was enacted that thereafter
whoever should have an "use, confidence, or trust" in
any hereditaments should be "deemed and adjudged in
lawful seisin, estate, and possession" for the same estate
that he had in use; that is, that he should become,
instead of the feoffees or trustees, the full legal owner
(or, more exactly, feudal tenant) for all purposes, and
that the absence of any actual delivery of possession to
him should make no difference. Here this brief statement must suffice; there are, in fact, subsidiary provisions of some length to work out and safeguard the
general idea. The result was as follows. If Stanford made a feoffment to More, Fisher, and Brooke,
to hold to the use of himself, the statute made this
ineffectual. Before the statute, More, Fisher, and
Brooke would have become the only tenants whom the

---

[1] Observe that fines and recoveries are put on a level with feoffments as common and recognised forms of conveying land. It
is only the "subtil practised" conveyance to secret uses that is
aimed at.

common law courts could notice, and the only persons
liable for the feudal dues (which, however, would mostly
never become demandable), while the Court of Chancery
would compel them to allow Stanford all the benefit
of the estate. By the operation of the statute, More,
Fisher, and Brooke would not become owners at all;
Stanford, by being named to take the use, would at once
come into their place. He would be as much the legal
tenant as before, and liable to all the legal burdens and
incidents. A feoffment to John, or to John and William
or to John and William and Peter, to the use of Peter,
or in trust or confidence for Peter, was made by the
statute equivalent to a feoffment to Peter. The use
carried with it the legal estate; in the curious technical
phrase which has ever since been current in the books,
the use was said to be executed in Peter by the statute.
And the law thus made by the Statute of Uses is law
to this day.

Yet the statute ultimately failed in every one of its
chief objects. It abolished wills of land (though, oddly
enough, not in direct terms); but so unpopular was the
restriction [1] that a few years later (1540) an Act was
passed expressly enabling tenants in fee simple to dispose by will of two-thirds of the land held by them in
military tenure, and the whole of that held in socage.
The statute was not improbably meant to put an end to
new-fangled modifications of ownership by allowing no
conveyance to take effect which would not have been

---

[1] The repeal of the Statute of Uses was one of the articles of
redress of grievances put forward by the leaders of the Pilgrimage
of Grace in 1536. See the documents ap. Froude, *Hist. Eng.* iii.
91, 105, 158

good at common law;[1] but it was interpreted by practice
and in time by the courts as giving full legal validity
to all interests which could formerly have been created
by way of use, and would have been protected by the
Chancellor.   All that the jealousy of the common
lawyers could effect was to saddle this new licence of
disposition with certain qualifications of a highly technical and irrational kind.   Again, it was intended that
there should be no use or confidence without legal
ownership.   But some ingenious person bethought him
that the statute had provided only for one transfer or
"execution" of the legal possession to couple it with
the use.   There was no denying that a conveyance to
John to the use of Peter gave Peter the legal estate.
But what if the conveyance was to John, to the use of
Peter, to the use of Paul?   It was not only argued, but
decided and settled, that the bidding of the statute was
satisfied, or as was then said, its operation was exhausted, in making Peter the legal owner.   Paul had
"a use upon a use"; this interest, it was held, was
beyond the scope of the statute, and must be left, like
uses before the statute, to the protection and management of the Court of Chancery.   "An use," said the
judges, "cannot be engendered of an use."[2]   In like
manner if Thomas, tenant in fee simple, conveyed to
John and his heirs to the use of Thomas for his life,

---

[1] Both Coke and Bacon appear to have thought so.   The fact
that the statute wholly omits to say anything which could fairly
be so construed goes, at that time, for very little.

[2] It is difficult to appreciate this reason.   Perhaps it was made
plausible by its analogy to the familiar (and then commonly
received) argument against usury, that it is against nature for
money to beget money.

and after his death to the use of Peter and his heirs, in trust to perform Thomas's last will, and then by his will declared that Robert and his heirs should have the land,—here after Thomas's death Peter had an estate in fee simple, and Robert had no title at all in a common law court; he could only compel Peter in the Court of Chancery to let him enjoy the land, or deal with it according to his direction. In technical terms, Robert had an equitable estate, but no legal estate. Thus the Chancellor's jurisdiction, so far from being cut short, was fortified and enlarged; and uses and trusts, instead of being "extirped," flourished all the more in a new form. The word trust became appropriated, as it still is, for these uses of the second order which the statute leaves untouched. We commonly hear and speak of lands being conveyed to the use of A in trust for B; the distinction is so fixed in practice and so convenient that nobody would think of neglecting it, but still it is matter of convenience only. "In trust for A" or "in confidence for A," followed by "to the use of B," would have exactly the same effect.

Once more, among the mischiefs to be remedied by the statute was the secrecy of conveyances, which had been introduced through uses. The open ceremony of "livery of seisin" was to be restored to its full value, as pointing out the real owner; and in those days of sparse population and little migration, when every man knew his neighbours and their doings, it was no doubt as good a means of securing publicity as any register could have been. But how did the statute operate? By one masterful stroke, against all principle formerly recognised, it turned the possessor in use into a legal possessor;

and there were other ways besides actual conveyance to feoffees in trust by which uses might be created before the statute. In particular, if Brooke agreed with Fitzherbert to sell him a piece of land, and Fitzherbert paid the agreed price, it was the rule of the Court of Chancery that Brooke was bound in conscience not only to make a proper legal conveyance to Fitzherbert, but forthwith to let him have all the advantages of ownership. By the "bargain and sale" (such was the accustomed term) Fitzherbert acquired the use or equitable interest in the land. If, then, the bargain and sale were made after the statute came into force, Fitzherbert would get the legal interest also; he must be "deemed and adjudged in lawful seisin, estate, and possession." That is, the full legal ownership of land would be transferred from one man to another by acts which might be strictly private, need not be recorded in writing, and might be incapable of legal proof.[1] So manifest a danger did not escape notice. It was seen that without fresh legislative precaution lands might pass from one to another "on payment of a little money in an alehouse," as one or two of the old books say. In the same year with the Statute of Uses an Act was passed to the effect that no estate of inheritance or freehold, or any use thereof, should be conveyed by bargain and sale, unless the bargain and sale was made by deed, and the deed enrolled[2] within

---

[1] At that time and long afterwards parties could not be witnesses in a court of common law.

[2] An enrolment is an official copy made on a roll of parchment. Before 1849 the authentic text of Acts of Parliament was the engrossment on the Parliament Roll: now a copy printed on vellum has taken the place of this.

six months either in one of the courts at Westminster
or in the county where the land lay. This was intended to provide, and did provide for some time, that
land should be dealt with either by feoffment, by the
still more solemn "matter of record," or by deeds
publicly registered. But the invention of lawyers was
at length too much for the precautions of Parliament.
The Statute of Enrolments had nothing to say of estates
less than freehold, such as a term of years. Interests
for a term of years (of which more in their place under
the head of Landlord and Tenant) had become familiar;
and probably the makers of the statute thought it unnecessary and impracticable to impose the formality
and expense of an enrolled deed on farmers' tenancies.
Here, however, was an unsuspected loophole. It was
discovered that since the Statute of Uses a bargain and
sale by Dyer (having the freehold), to Anderson, suppose, for the term of one year, put Anderson in the
same position as if he had actually entered on the land;
for by the words of the statute he was to be "deemed
in lawful possession." Now a tenant in possession
could acquire the freehold by a simple deed (called a
release) from the owner of the reversion. Livery of
seisin could not be given to one already in possession,
and the fact of possession (which by the old law implied
an actual entry) was thought to supply the notoriety of
a feoffment. In the present case Dyer, the day after
making the bargain and sale for one year, would grant
by release to Anderson, who was now in constructive
possession by the Statute of Uses, his remaining interest
or reversion in the freehold. Thus Anderson might
become tenant in fee simple without any publicity at

all, and the Statute of Enrolments was evaded. This process was called a conveyance by lease and release, and was the common method of transferring freehold lands for more than two centuries. Doubts were for some time entertained as to its validity, but by 1630 the point was considered no longer open to discussion.

Thus was the secrecy of modern English conveyancing established. Its lines were fixed by the results of the Statute of Uses, and what legislation has done since amounts to little more than the simplifying of its formal elements. "A system of infinite subtlety, but answering, it must be acknowledged, most important purposes, has been framed upon this Statute, while most of the evils which it was meant to remedy remain." [1] The frauds and other mischiefs which our ancestors, not without reason, apprehended have been in part provided against by the systematic development and refinement of the jurisdiction of the Court of Chancery, and in part by the ingenuity of counsellors. In the course of the seventeenth and eighteenth centuries conveyancers worked out a system of private investigation of titles which is still in use, and which, though exceedingly [2] cumbrous and expensive, is fairly effectual. One can only say fairly effectual, for there remain possibilities of fraud which no ordinary precaution can exclude, and from time to time great hardship is thereby caused to persons who have laid out their money in good faith and have not failed in any point of due diligence.

Other causes too were at work to break up the

<hr>

[1] *First Report of Real Property Commissioners*, p. 8.
[2] I should have said intolerably, but for the fact that land owners have so long tolerated it.

feudal scheme of land law.   The military services were
obsolete.   Spain was teaching the world the power of
disciplined standing armies, and the growing use of
firearms brought in a need of copious and uniform
munitions of war such as the old assize of arms [1] could
not meet.   Warlike equipment and organisation were
henceforth more and more to be the immediate charge
of the State.   In this and other ways the feudal tenures
had lost their original significance ; and the money payments to the Crown and other lords appeared no longer
as natural incidents of tenure, but as vexatious burdens
on the full dominion of an owner.   Even the fact that
the decrease in the value of money had already greatly
lessened such of them as were set at fixed amounts
operated, we may well think, in the same direction.
The same man who as tenant would cheerfully pay a
substantial rent will, as soon as he regards himself as
owner, resent the payment of much lighter but apparently casual and arbitrary demands.   Then the
besetting ambition of lordship, "an excess of will in
men's minds, affecting to have assurances of their estates
and possessions to be revocable in their own times, and
too irrevocable after their own times,"[2] was all the more
stimulated ; nor did professional astuteness fail to devise
the means of satisfying it.   How the feudal tenants of
England were definitely made real owners, and how the
licence of disposition and posthumous control which the

---

[1] Sundry statutes and ordinances known by this name enjoined
all freemen to keep in readiness a contribution of warlike weapons
and equipment, which was graduated according to their rank.

[2] Bacon, *Reading on the Statute of Uses* (Works, vii. 409, ed.
Spedding).

Statute of Uses seemed to make unlimited was, met by
the baffled legislature but by a fresh exercise of judicial
power, confined within certain though liberal bounds,
shall be told in the following chapter.   The Statute of
Uses marks the close of the medieval epoch, and intro-
duces a time of transition during which a new system
works itself out, a system which after the Restoration is
continued without any notable break down to our time.
A landmark so prominent and so memorable demands a
pause before we pass on.

CHAPTER V

DEVELOPMENT OF THE MODERN LAW

THE century that followed the passing of the Statute of Uses was a time of great legal activity in all directions. During the latter half of the sixteenth and the first half of the seventeenth centuries the books were produced which, for most practical purposes, have long been regarded as the ultimate evidence of English Common Law. Coke's Commentary upon *Littleton's Tenures*, eminent in the charmed (and long since closed)[1] circle of "books of authority," was published in 1628. About the same time began the publication of printed reports of judicial arguments and decisions, a kind of publication which has gone on increasing till it has now swollen to a vast and unmanageable bulk. The advice of Coke to students, that "it is ever good to rely upon the book at large," has become a precept beyond human powers to fulfil, and the text-books of special subjects which digest and methodise the matter of the reports are themselves groaning under the burden. But in

[1] Sir Michael Foster's *Discourse of Crown Law* (1762) was, I think, the latest addition. Blackstone, and some few later books, come very near, but only near, to being authoritative in the technical sense.

those days lawyers had more leisure. They found time
to debate fully all the points of interest raised by a
case, whether the solution of them was necessary for
the actual decision or not ; and, with all their pedantry
and occasional perversity of intellect, they held fast to
a high and serious conception of the profession they
followed, and their duty to it as a science and an art,
which the modern practitioner must for the most part
be content to envy. The law of real property got its
full share of the discussion and development that went
on in this period. Yet the results of the Statute of
Uses were long in ripening. Indeed the final touch
was not put to them till the year 1833, on the very
eve of the modern period of reform, when the limits of
the "rule against perpetuities" were settled by the
House of Lords. Practically, however, the structure
of family settlements of land had assumed its modern
form before the Restoration, and the practice of conveyancers became, from the seventeenth century onwards, a fixed and well understood routine, improved
in details from time to time by addition or variation,
but preserving its main points unchanged.

The general scheme of a "strict settlement" is of this
kind. Let A be a living landowner who has a living
son B, and wishes to keep his estate "in the family" as
long as possible. For simplicity's sake, we will suppose
A to be tenant in fee simple to begin with. A conveyance is executed by which A becomes tenant for life,
and B tenant for life after A's death ; or else A by his
will makes B the first tenant for life. Then an estate
tail (generally in tail male) is given to the first son of
B—a person not yet in existence, and who may never

come into existence ; and similar estates are given to B's
second and other sons in succession. Each of these dispositions can take effect only if every previous estate tail
fails to begin, or comes to its natural end, by persons
entitled to it not existing or ceasing to exist. Thus if
the estates are in tail male, and B has three sons, the
third son, or any of his descendants in the male line,
can become tenant in tail only if the two elder sons and
all their descendants in the male line, if any, are dead,
and none of them has exercised his power of barring the
entail—a power of which no tenant in tail can by any
device whatever be deprived. There will follow, probably, similar dispositions in favour of B's sons in tail
general, so as to admit their descendants in the female
line after those in the male line ; then other and somewhat less elaborate ones in favour of B's daughters ;
then, again, A's children other than B, if he has any,
and their possible descendants,[1] and also (in the case of
a settlement made in A's lifetime) A's children who may
yet be born, are provided for in a series of successive
"limitations" of the same type as those already described. In the remote contingency of all these dispositions running their full course till every specified line of
descent is exhausted, the ultimate "remainder" (see p.
81 above) is usually declared to be for A's "right heirs,"
that is, the person or persons who, at the time when the
previous interests have been worked out, may answer
the description of A's heir according to the common
course of descent of a fee-simple estate.

---

[1] It is a question of detail, on which the practice varies according
to the desire of parties in the particular case, whether the descendants in the male line of the settlor's younger children are postponed
or preferred to descendants in the female line of the elder ones.

This may seem pretty complicated, but it is the least complicated part of a modern settlement. Practically it is only in rare cases that the remoter interests are carefully mapped out ever owns into possession. If all things happen as is desired, the regular course is this:— B becomes tenant for life on A's death. He has a son C (born either during A's life or afterwards, it matters not which), who is "tenant in tail in remainder." English lawyers do not say that he will be tenant in tail when the life tenancy comes to a end, but that he is tenant in tail subject to B's life estate. Suppose that C comes of age in B's lifetime. He can now without B's consent bar the entail as against his own issue, but not as against those "in remainder"; in other words, he can neither sell nor borrow to much purpose, for a title depending on the continuance of his descendants, which is all he can give to a purchaser or lender, is a precarious and speculative thing.[1] This check on C's power of alienation is a result of the technical necessities of the old "common recovery," which could not be carried through to its full effect without the aid of the person in actual possession of the freehold. When fines and recoveries were abolished in 1833, a new but substantially equivalent check was provided by the Legislature, the purpose of

---

[1] The curious kind of estate created by the conveyance in fee simple of a tenant in tail not in possession, without the concurrence of the owners of estates preceding his own, is called a base fee. Though uncommon, it is not unknown in practice, and it has been used by George Eliot in Felix Holt, with great effect and with perfect correctness, as part of the machinery of the plot; insomuch that conveyancers reading the novel have been known to lament seriously, as if the thing had happened to one of their own clients, that the parties did not take better advice.

that measure being only to simplify the form of proceeding and put an end to fictions and useless expense. Since that date B would be "protector of the settlement," and his consent to any disposition by C is an express and direct condition for its validity against the ulterior interests created by the settlement. B then stands in a commanding position towards C; B and C between them are masters of the estate, while C alone can do very little, and B alone—except in the extraordinary contingency of all the subsequent limitations failing—can do nothing beyond the term of his own life. And when B proposes that C, in consideration of being adequately provided for during the rest of B's life, shall join in making a new settlement in which C shall be only a tenant for life, and other successive limited interests shall be laid out in the same fashion as in the former one, but with C and C's issue in the place of B and B's issue, there is not much probability that C can or will refuse. This process is repeated, as occasion serves, from generation to generation; and so long as it can be kept up the estate is never in the hands of an absolute owner.[1]

Hence arose the necessity for the further complicated machinery which, as already hinted, must be added to these dispositions: I speak for the moment without regard to recent legislation, of which more in its due place afterwards. If things stood merely as now de-

---

[1] The process of settling and resettling family estates has repeatedly been described in forms intended to be more or less intelligible to the lay public. I have purposely written my own account without referring to any other; not that I can hope to be more successful than my predecessors.

scribed, there would be no provision made out of the
estate for the younger branches of the family (save in
the remotely contingent event of some of them coming
into possession of the whole), and no means of making
any. Neither would there be any means of effecting a
sale or exchange of any part of the settled estate, granting leases, or exercising many other necessary and usual
functions of an owner, during the minority of a tenant
in tail. And here the wide and flexible applications of
the Statute of Uses (undreamt of by its authors) come
in. It would be possible, indeed, without the aid of the
statute, to effect most of the purposes of a modern
settlement, if not all, by conveying the whole estate to
trustees in the first instance, who would, like feoffees
before the statute, have the legal fee simple, or, in other
words, would be the only persons whom a court of
common law would recognise as owners. Such a course
might nowadays be viewed with equanimity by lawyers
and landowners, and in fact it is sometimes adopted in
settlements made by will. But two centuries or even
one century ago there was still a kind of magic in men's
apprehension about the "legal estate." It is still true
in strictness of theory that an "equitable estate," as we
call the interest of a person beneficially entitled under a
trust, is not perfect ownership—a right available against
all the world—but is only a right to claim the profits and
enjoyment of ownership from the determinate person
who is the trustee. The beneficiary is in the same
position as the old "cestui que use" before the Statute
of Uses. Increased security has been given to this kind
of interest by the full but gradual development of the
jurisdiction and jurisprudence of the Court of Chancery;

the trustee's obligation being extended to all persons
deriving or claiming title through him otherwise than
for value, in good faith, and with due diligence of
inquiry.　This process was still in its youth at the time
of the Restoration, and it may well be thought that
nothing less than the power given by the Statute of Uses
to devise complex modifications of the legal ownership
itself would have sufficed to strengthen the hands and
embolden the invention of Orlando Bridgman and his
contemporaries.[1]　Broadly speaking, there are two kinds
of objects for which the special powers and provisions
now in question are introduced : the benefit and support
of wives and younger children of the successive holders
of the estate, and the general management of the estate
for the advantage of all parties interested in its profits.
These objects are effected partly by the action of the
person for the time being in possession, partly by the
intervention of trustees named for that end in the settlement itself, and through an ingenious and intricate
machinery which is far too artificial to be described
here.　It is enough to say that the machine has been
brought to great technical perfection by the experience
of about two centuries, and, when constructed by a
skilful artist who takes advantage of all known improvements, works with much less friction than might be
expected.　On the other hand, if the workmanship is
not first-rate to begin with (and for various reasons—

---

[1] Orlando Bridgman, who gained great fame as a conveyancer
before and during the Commonwealth time, and was afterwards
Lord Keeper, is credited with the invention of the "strict settlement" in substantially its present form, avoiding certain risks to
which it had before his time been subject.

haste, ignorance of country practitioners, or what not—it often falls short of this standard), very serious trouble may ensue. With regard to the special trustees just mentioned, it must not be supposed that they exercise much discretion of their own. As a rule, they are little more than wheels in the machine, the management of which is in the hands of the family solicitor, fortified at need by the opinion and advice of counsel. It would be considered meddlesome if they offered to exercise their powers before they were asked. At the same time they are fully answerable for what is done by them on the usual request and advice; and they are mostly persons of such weight and standing as to be above suspicion of conniving at any reckless or improper dealings with the settled estate. In short, the trustees of a family settlement are something like the constitutional safeguards of a complex political system; their presence is, in ordinary circumstances, hardly perceived, but they hold great powers in reserve, which may be used with effect on an emergency.

The parallel just now suggested is not a casual one. There is nothing, perhaps, in the institutions of modern Europe which comes so near to an *imperium in imperio* as the settlement of a great English estate. The settlor is a kind of absolute lawgiver for two generations; his will suspends for that time the operation of the common law of the land, and substitutes for it an elaborate constitution of his own making. These constitutions are in fact all modelled on the same, or very nearly the same, type; for the desire of great landowners has constantly been to make the strictest settlements which the law would allow, and the law, as we shall immediately see, has set bounds, though liberal ones, to the power of fettering inheritances and suspending absolute ownership. And the ingenuity of conveyancers, devising how to satisify private ambition to the utmost within the field left clear to it by public ordinance, has produced that curious and exquisite structure which, a hundred years hence, will probably be as much abandoned to the care of a few legal antiquaries as the learning of remitter and collateral warranty. But a correction is needed when we speak of the family settlement as a constitution ; for though it resembles a modern political system in its multiplication of checks and counter-checks, and in the tacit or half-expressed understandings by which its working is made practicable, there is another respect in which it is more fitly compared to the customs of an Oriental despotism. When the authors of a settlement have once made their disposition, it is like the law of the Medes and Persians rather than the acts of a modern legislature. They are as powerless as the great king of old to alter their decrees, unless they have made special provisions for that purpose which are not usually made in practice, and which indeed would be inconsistent with the main object of making the estate as a whole as nearly inalienable as possible.

It might be a topic of curious meditation for the student of comparative jurisprudence to note how well the English landowning families have striven, though all unconsciously, to reproduce in our modern society something like the image of an archaic Aryan household. There is at the head of all the eldest living male ancestor, revered by his descendants and inferiors, and exercising great control and influence in divers ways,

and yet with his power over the family property strictly
limited—in the ancient household by custom, in its
modern counterpart by accustomed convention. There
are the women and younger generations of the family,
subject to the house-father in one sense, and yet having
rights in the common inheritance which he cannot interfere with. The free dependents, not members of the
family, who swelled the state and substance of the
ancient household, may well enough be represented by
the modern tenant-farmers. Only the highest and
lowest extremes of the community are wanting. Slavery
and serfdom are happily long since extinct in our land ;
and so are the rites of the domestic altar, which were
for the ancient Aryan family the bond of fellowship, the
assurance of the departed ancestors' welfare, and the
pledge of their favour to the living. Some brilliant
theorists have sought in these the very origin of property and inheritance ; and to this day the worship of
household gods and ancestors is in full force in India,
and lies at the foundation of the law which English
judges administer to the Queen's Hindu subjects. The
most fearful imprecation by which a Hindu can bind
himself is that, if he speak falsely, he may have no son
to deliver his soul from hell by due performance of the
sacrifice. But hardly can a faint survival of such old-
world usage (though much of the abiding human passions
which only change their garment from age to age) be
traced by the modern observer's fancy in an English
estate. He may speculate on a remote connection of
Pitris and Lares with the domestic chaplain, the an-
cestral monuments in the parish church, or the family
pew. Or, when he notes who is now the real possessor

of the secrets of the estate, the real familiar spirit at whose bidding the magical powers of the settlement are called forth, and without whose aid no matter of weight can be undertaken, he may peradventure dream that "the disestablished Lar," to use the term of a late ingenious writer,[1] is not dead but transformed, and lives embodied in the family solicitor.

We have said that the modern form of settlement dates, roundly speaking, from the Restoration. But already in the sixteenth century, when controversy was keen about Uses and the effect of the great statute, lawyers had an inkling of what was coming. And their opinions of the invidiousness and social inconvenience of strict settlements (or even of dispositions falling far short of what we now understand by the term) were such as would not many years ago have been called Radical. Coke has been quoted in the last chapter. Let us hear Bacon :—

"First [it is said] that [it is a wisdom and foresight for every man to imagine of that which may happen to his posterity, and by all ways establish his name. To this I answer that it is a wisdom, but a greater than even Solomon aspired after, who had a large heart, as the Scripture saith. For I find that he uses other language, when he says that he must leave the fruit of his labour to one of whom he does not know if he shall be a fool or a wise man. And yet does he say that he shall be an usufructuary or tenant restrained in a perpetuity? No ; but the absolute lord of all that he had by his travail. So little did he know of these establishments." . . .

Whether Solomon had any land by his travail, in the

_____
[1] Hearn, *The Aryan Household.*

modern sense of having a thing in absolute ownership,
we need not stop to inquire. As king he was no doubt,
in a sense, lord of the soil of his kingdom ; but, if he
was like other eastern kings, he could not lawfully dis-
possess the meanest of his subjects who duly paid the
customary revenue. Private ownership of land, at any
rate, has been of slow growth in the East. Under the
ancient rule of custom which is slowly decaying before
our eyes in India the land belonged to the village or to
the family, and was inalienable, though the possession
and enjoyment might change hands within the circle of
joint owners. The Hindu joint family is the true and
ancient perpetuity. Later attempts at founding perpetuities by way of entail, *majorat*, strict settlement, and
the like, are the rebellion of a privileged class against
the tendency of the civilised world towards absolute
and several ownership, even as the schemes of Socialists
and other visionary reformers for " Land Nationalisation," or whatever else it may be called, are the rebellion
of those for whom the education of the world goes too
slowly, and who vainly seek a charm that shall redress
in one instant the balance of life between rich and poor.
But Bacon has more to say to us. Let us hear him
further :—

   " Some young heir when he first comes to the float
of his living outcompasseth himself in expenses, yet
perhaps in good time reclaims himself, and has a desire
to recover his estate ; but has no readier way than to
sell a parcel to free himself from the biting and con-
suming interest. But now he cannot redeem himself
with his proper means, and though he be reclaimed in
mind, yet can he not remedy his estate.

" So, passing over the considerations of humanity, let us now consider the discipline of families. And touching this I will speak in modesty and under correction. Though I reverence the laws of my country, yet I observe one defect in them ; and that is, there is no footstep of the reverend *potestas patria* which was so commended in ancient times. . . . This only yet remains : if the father has any patrimony and the son be disobedient, he may disinherit him ; if he will not deserve his blessing, he shall not have his living. But this device of perpetuities has taken this power from the father likewise and has tied and made subject (as the proverb is) the parents to their cradle, and so notwithstanding he has the curse of his father, yet he shall have the land of his grandfather." [1]

The term perpetuity, as here used by Bacon, and constantly used by modern lawyers, signifies a disposition which attempts to make property inalienable beyond certain limits fixed, or conceived as being fixed, by the general law. What, then, are those limits? It was long before they were ascertained. In Bacon's time, and for a century later, the legal question was still open to be argued on wide grounds of policy. There was no obvious limit to the time within which trusts, or dispositions operating under the Statute of Uses, might be calculated to take effect. Yet it was felt that a limit there must be. It was agreed that "the rules of the law to prevent perpetuities are the polity of the kingdom," but nobody knew what the rules were. A long series of experiments, extending into the second quarter

---

[1] Arguments in Chudleigh's case. Works, vol. vii. pp. 632-35, ed. Spedding.

of the eighteenth century, determined the limits of safety
for founders of families.   Yet another century passed
before the rule was finally settled in all points.   In
order to understand the form which it took, we must
go back to the older law.   Quite apart from the learning of Uses, it was possible, at any time after the statute
De Donis,[1] to grant by one and the same conveyance an
estate for life, say in the manor of Dale, to Markham ;
and, subject to his life interest, an estate tail to Martin ;
after the determination of that estate another estate tail
to Newton, and so on through any number of persons,
till some one was named to take an ultimate fee simple,
after which there was nothing more to dispose of.
Martin, being of full age, could at any time, but not
without Markham's concurrence while Markham's life
estate was in existence, "suffer a recovery," in the
manner explained in the last chapter, and thus acquire
and dispose of the fee simple, when all the subsequent
dispositions made by the original grant would go for
nothing.   So far, then, the manor is inalienable until
Markham's life estate ceases, or Martin, if an infant at
the date of the original conveyance, is twenty-one years
old, whichever of these events happens latest.   But it
was not necessary that Martin, a person in existence,
should be named as the successor after the first life
estate.   After some doubt[2] it was settled that an estate
for life might be given to Markham, and an estate "in
remainder" for life, in tail, or in fee, to Markham's first
son, though at the time of the gift he had no son.   The

[1] The legal reader will remember that a remainder over could
not be limited upon a fee simple conditional at common law.
[2] Digby, *History of Law of Real Property*, c. 5, § 3.

series of dispositions which form the groundwork of a
modern settlement, as above described, are only the full
application of this principle. But it was not, and is not,
allowable to give an estate for life to Markham's first
son, after that another estate for life to the first son of
that son, and so following—by which means, if allowed,
the estate might have been made inalienable for an
indefinite time.   The title could not be secured for
Markham's descendants in the male line further than by
giving an estate tail to his first son ; nor indeed was
the security perfect even so far, for if no son was in
existence at the date of the settlement it was still in the
father's power to destroy the "contingent remainder,"
which, when a son was born, would become "vested"
in him and beyond the father's control.   Suppose a son
born and his interest unimpaired.   That son might
possibly be born in the last year of Markham's life,
or even some months after his death.   In that case
twenty-one years might elapse from Markham's death
before any one had power to alien the fee simple of the
manor.   But whenever a tenant in tail of full age is in
possession, he can dispose of the fee simple notwithstanding any attempt made by the terms of the settlement to prohibit or restrain him.   So it comes to this,
that the furthest period until which alienation can be
restrained by settlement, apart from provisions taking
effect by way of use or trust, is the end of twenty-one
years, and exceptionally something more, after the
death of some person living at the date when the settlement is made.

Now uses and trusts were not directly amenable to
these rules.   Being originally nothing else than direc-

tions to the "feoffees to uses"[1] to allow the profits of
the land to be enjoyed by persons named by the feoffor,
or to be ascertained in the manner pointed out by him,
which directions were enforced by the Chancellor as
binding on the feoffee's conscience, they had nothing to
do with the rules of the common law as to the creation
of estates. These newly-modelled interests might,
under cover of the feoffee's legal possession, be made to
shift about in the most capricious fashion. By the
common law Fortescue could not give an estate to
Brian and his heirs so long as they should use the name
and arms of Fortescue, and if they did not, then to
some one else. But when uses were established Fortescue might infeoff Moyle and his heirs to the use of
Brian and his heirs until any of them should cease to
use the name and arms of Fortescue, and then to the
use of Prisot and his heirs. And as far as theory
went, the contingency might have been something
wholly unconnected with the estate and beyond the
parties' control — for example, until Herne's oak in
Windsor Park should fall, or until a new Pope should
take the name of Leo. There were other contrivances,
more complex in form but similar in principle, by
which like results could be produced for a variety of
purposes.[2]

[1] P. 94, above.
[2] "Uses of this class," said a learned and accurate modern
writer (William Hayes, *Momentary View*, etc., 1840, a. 31), "may
be described as altogether eccentric; as deviating from the course
prescribed by the original laws of the system, not without considerable disturbance of its ordinary operations." It is said that
by common law "a man may have an inheritance in fee simple in
lands, as long as such a tree shall grow, because a man may have

Neither the judges who had broken through the express terms of the statute *De Donis*, nor the successors who inherited their tradition, could be expected to tolerate this new-found way of fettering the possession and inheritance of lands. And, in fact, there was not (what one might look for) a crowd of daring attempts to push forward to all lengths in that course, but settlors of estates rather felt their way step by step till it was known how far they might venture; so little doubt was there that the Courts would once more hold themselves authorised by the general "policy of the law" to make new law for a new mischief. The rule was at last settled by analogy (an analogy more felt than expressed) to the course of the common law. Not without sundry fluctuations of both opinion and judicial decision, it came to be understood, towards the middle of the eighteenth century, that a disposition of any kind of property [1] intended to take effect in the future must be so framed as necessarily to take effect, if at all, after a lapse of time not exceeding twenty-one years from the death of some certain person, or of the survivor of certain persons, who are living at the date of the settlement if it is made by deed, or at the date of the testator's death if it is made by will. As late as 1833 it was decided by the House of Lords that those twenty-one years need not have reference to the infancy

---

an inheritance in the tree itself" (*Liford's* case, 11 Co. Rep. 49a). This raises a very curious and difficult question, on which the learned reader is referred to Note G. In any case, a remainder over could not be limited after such an estate.

[1] The rule is not confined to land, though we now have to do with it only in that application.

of any person.   In particular cases the rule of law which
treats an unborn child as a person in existence for all
purposes of his benefit may have the effect of adding some
months to the time allowed.   A disposition which goes
beyond these limits is said to be "bad for perpetuity."
Thus a gift to the first child of A (having at the time
no children) who shall attain the age of twenty-one
years, or to all his children who shall attain that age, is
valid.   A gift to the first son of A who shall attain the
age of twenty-five years is of no effect, and it makes no
difference that A may in fact have a son who attains
that age in his own lifetime.   Again, a gift by will to
the first person who shall climb up the cross of St.
Paul's after the testator's death is "void for remoteness," though somebody may peradventure do the thing
within a week ; if the gift were to the first person who
should so climb within twenty-one years after the
testator's death, it would be good.

The rule, it must be well marked, does not prevent
an estate in remainder or reversion from being made
expectant on an interest which may, or which naturally
will, endure for a much longer time.   For English
lawyers regard an estate in remainder or reversion not
as a future interest, but as a present interest subject
to the "particular estate" which together with the remainder or reversion makes up the fee simple.   To
illustrate this by common cases :—If Holt grants an
estate tail to Powell, with remainder to Finch in fee,
Finch has the fee simple subject to Powell's estate tail,
and can dispose of his interest at once, though it is uncertain when it may take effect by the failure of Powell's
heirs under the entail, or whether (since Powell or any

of his successors can bar the entail and acquire the whole fee simple) it will take effect at all. Holt will be in the same position if, instead of granting the fee simple subject to the estate tail as a *remainder*, he keeps it as his *reversion ;* he can at once deal with it for what it is worth as he thinks fit. Again, Bayley grants a lease to Buller for ninety-nine years. If Bayley tries to provide that at the end of the ninety-nine years the person who is then his eldest living male descendant shall have the land, this is "void for remoteness," as the creation of an interest to take effect after the lapse of more than twenty-one years. But if he leaves it alone, he has a perfectly good reversion by the common law, which he may dispose of now or hereafter as he thinks fit, no less than if it were land in his actual possession. If he sells, it is commonly said that he sells the ground-rent; but in legal conception and language he sells the land itself subject to the lease; and if the lease were for a thousand years, the legal doctrine would be the same.

Such is in outline the "rule against perpetuities," which, as regards these general principles, is now a settled part of our law. Many curious questions might still be raised on the application of it in various circumstances; but the skilled and cautious routine of conveyancers is for the most part, though not invariably, successful in keeping clear of them. Certain points in the legal theory are also still unsettled, or have been settled only in the last few years, but it would be unprofitable to explain or discuss them here.[1]

The rule prevents property from being made certainly

[1] See Note G, on Settlements and Perpetuity.

inalienable beyond the limits of time fixed by it. But it would not be correct to say that the property must therefore be in fact alienable when the restrictive dispositions have run their full course. There must then be some person absolutely entitled, but that person may be an infant or a lunatic, so that yet another generation may elapse before there is an owner with full and active power of disposal.

The questions thus decided arose for the most part upon dispositions by will. The Statute of Uses, as we saw, was intended to make the devise [1] of land by will thenceforth impossible; but the prohibition gave so much offence as to be soon removed, though for the time to a limited extent only, by the Statute of Wills of Henry VIII. (p. 102 above). And it was held that, dispositions by will being once allowed, either the Statute of Uses or its analogy (it matters not which) was applicable in their favour. Thus a man could, and he still can, by his last will, as well as by acts executed in his lifetime, create interests unknown and indeed repugnant to the doctrine of the old common law. Persons making wills are notoriously more adventurous and capricious than those who make settlements to take effect in their lifetime; in part, it may be, because the obscurity or perplexity of their directions can vex only posterity; moreover, they are less under the influence

---

[1] A gift by will of freehold land, or of such rights arising out of or connected with land as are by English law classed with it as *real property*, is called a *devise*. A gift by will of personal property (a term including leasehold as well as movable property) is called a *bequest*. Dispositions of real property of a kind not conforming to the rules of the common law before the Statute of Uses are called, when made by will, *executory devises*.

K

of discreet advisers. Hence dispositions by will produced much the greater part of the litigation which
defined the bounds of legal control over future generations.

Complete freedom of dealing with land by will was
a result of the abolition of military tenures, an event
which preceded in time the settlement of the rule
against perpetuities, and may be taken as marking the
full close of the medieval stage of the law. Though in
form it stands as one of the first acts of the Restoration,
in substance it was one of the many law reforms undertaken in the time of the Commonwealth. Most of those
reforms were rejected or dropped at the Restoration.
This one was too popular and necessary to be so dealt
with; nor was unexceptionable authority wanting, for a
similar measure had been strongly advocated by Coke.[1]
The Act of the first Parliament of Charles II. for
abolishing the military tenures and their incidents was
passed in 1660. No notice was taken by it of the
previous Act of the Commonwealth which had been
passed in 1656, all statutes of the Commonwealth being
treated under the restored monarchy as made without
lawful authority, and mere nullities; but the same provisions were enacted in a rather more elaborate form.[2]
All freehold tenures were reduced to the one type of
"free and common socage,"[3] with an important twofold

[1] See the details and references in Mr. Digby's *History*, ch. ix.
It is a great error, but it has been a common one, to overlook these
facts, and regard the legislation of 1660 as an arrangement between
Charles II. and the great landowners.

[2] According to Madox (*Hist. Exch.*, i. 620, ed. 1769), the workmanship of the statute leaves much to be desired.

[3] See pp. 59 and 63, above.

result. First, all the vexatious incidents of military tenure disappeared with the tenure itself; only ancient money rents might remain payable by the tenant, which already had . become, by the changes in the value of money since they were fixed, almost or altogether nominal. Next, inasmuch as the statute of 1540 had enabled tenants in fee simple to dispose by will of the whole of their socage lands, and socage was now made the only freehold tenure, the whole of the fee-simple land in the kingdom became disposable by will. Feudal tenancy was converted for all practical purposes into full ownership. The "honorary services of grand serjeanty," that is, services due to the Sovereign in person by the terms of the tenure, were exempted from abolition ; and tenure in frank-almoigne, by which the greater part of ecclesiastical lands were and still are held, was left untouched.[1]

It had been proposed at an earlier time to compensate the Crown for the loss of feudal dues by assessment of a fixed money rent on the enfranchised lands.[2] This method was not now adopted, but the excise duties which had been invented by the Long Parliament and renewed under the Commonwealth were granted to the King, "to the intent and purpose that his Majesty, his heirs and successors, may receive a full and ample recompense and satisfaction" for the feudal incidents, and for certain other profits and privileges abolished by the same Act. There is a not uncommon impression, I believe, that the land tax was imposed as part of, or in

---

[1] This, however, was not a real exception, for every non-military free tenure is tenure in socage.

[2] Coke, 4 Inst. 202.

connection with, the same transaction, and to make up to the public revenue for the income formerly received from the military tenants of the Crown. But this is not so; we first hear of the land tax in 1692, and then as part of a scheme for a general property tax.[1] The Land tax itself has now shrunk into relative insignificance beside Schedule A of the Income tax, which in our time is the real and effective tax on landed property for national as distinct from local purposes. It is a true property tax, being, unlike the tax on profits under Schedule D, assessed on the gross, not on the net value. And if any one thinks land does not bear its fair share of taxation, and wants to raise the question in a practical form, his proper course would be to propose a differential rate under Schedule A. But it is easier, and for some purposes more profitable, to put forth sounding generalities than to work out a definite plan.[2]

There were other branches of law relating to land which the development of the seventeenth and eighteenth centuries brought into substantially their present condition. Of these the law of mortgage is the most important. The power and practice of making a debtor's property, and especially immovable property, a security to the creditor for the payment of his debt, are well-nigh as old as the legal recognition and judicial enforcement of any rights of property whatever. The

[1] Appendix I. to Mr. G. Brodrick's *English Land and English Landlords* (by Mr. Humphreys-Owen).

[2] A landowner who keeps land in hand pays not only as owner under Schedule A, but also as occupier under Schedule B, whether he occupies for profit or not. I doubt whether this is generally understood.

reflection is trite that both parties gain—the creditor
by having security, the debtor because a secured
creditor can let him have money on easier terms.
Good security means low interest as certainly as high
interest means bad security. Certain reformers who
wish on economical grounds to abolish mortgage altogether must take, it seems to me, an extremely sanguine
view of the facility of making a radical change in the
convenience and the desires of mankind. The forms,
however, in which English law has given effect to this
all but universal practice have been singularly ill
chosen. Beginning with fictitious and impracticable
stringency, our practice has ended in a wide and
dangerous laxity, which breeds doubtful titles and
litigation, and is no small encouragement to fraud.
In the medieval period we meet with two ways of
giving land in security. One of these consists in
handing over possession to the creditor, who repays
himself out of the rents and profits. This is called in
Latin *vivum vadium*, in French *vif gage*, because the
pledge in the creditor's possession is, as it were, alive
for the debtor's benefit in working off the debt. In
English it is called a Welsh mortgage; in modern
practice it seldom or never occurs. The other and
prevailing method is a conditional sale of the land by
the debtor to the creditor. If the debtor repays the
money with interest to the creditor at a stated time,
the creditor must give him back the land; if not, it
remains the creditor's. And this is properly called
mortgage, *mortuum vadium*, in opposition to the "vif
gage," where the growing profits go to extinguish the
debt, because the profits of the land are, as it were,

dead to the debtor. It must be difficult for any one but a lawyer to believe that so clumsy an operation is to this day the regular means of securing a debt on land in England. It is true that its harsh meagreness was amplified by the judgments of the Court of Chancery into a full and elaborate system of rules, abounding even to overmuch caution in safeguards for the debtor. The terms of the transaction were—as they still appear to be—that the debtor must pay his money to get back the land (redeem it, in the technical phrase) at a stated time, generally six months after the date of the agreement, or it would become the creditor's absolute property. But the Chancellors laid down that, notwithstanding these terms, the debtor should be admitted to redeem after the set time had past. The right thus allowed him in the Court of Chancery was called an "equity of redemption." In other words, the jurisprudence of that Court, looking to the substance of the dealing between the parties and disregarding the form, treated the borrower as still the real owner of the land, and the land as only pledged for the lender's security. But a corresponding right had then to be given to the lender, his nominal right to deal with the land as owner being made useless. He might indeed take possession when the debtor failed to pay on the appointed day, but he did so at his peril; the Court held him strictly accountable to the debtor, so that the plight of a mortgagee in possession [1] is one of the most unenviable known to the law. Therefore a more just and convenient redress was given him. He was allowed,

---

[1] The borrower who pledges his land by way of mortgage is called a *mortgagor*; the lender who holds it in pledge is a *mortgagee*.

if he could not get payment of his debt after due notice,
to sue in Chancery, that the borrower might be ordered
to pay the principal and all arrears of interest, or in
default be "foreclosed of his equity of redemption,"
that is, no longer protected against the strict legal
consequences of his agreement according to its form.
This, however, was found expensive and tedious ; and
it became an almost universal practice to insert in the
deed special provisions enabling the mortgagee to sell
the land and repay himself out of the proceeds, if the
debt were not paid off on notice, or if the interest fell
into arrear for more than a certain time.   Recently
this "power of sale" has been conferred on mortgagees
by Act of Parliament, so as to supersede in ordinary
cases the necessity of expressly repeating the provisions
which had become well settled by usage.   Power has
also been given to the Court to order a sale of the
property instead of foreclosure.   Shortly, the result is
this :—A deed of mortgage means something very
different from what it says, but this has so long been
an understood thing that nobody is misled by it.   The
mortgagee never expects to be repaid on the day
nominally appointed for redemption (not uncommonly,
indeed, there is an express stipulation that the principal
shall not be paid off till after a certain number of years),
and the mortgagor's possession is safe as long as he pays
the interest punctually.

But the Court of Chancery embarked on other adven-
tures, and discovered new methods of encumbering land.
It was not enough to remodel the old mortgage into
accordance with present convenience and the real expec-
tation of the parties.   Nor was it enough to hold that a

beneficial owner who had not the "legal estate" might raise money on the security of his beneficial interest in the same manner as a legal tenant. It was held, first, that an agreement to give a mortgage was not a mere personal agreement, but operated as a charge on the land itself in the hands of any one who knew of it; and then that an "equitable mortgage" might be created without any written agreement at all. The latter step came about thus:—As the first thing required of an English landowner by any one dealing with him for the land is to produce his title-deeds, the handing over of the title-deeds to a creditor, pending the preparation of a formal security, is a fairly effectual precaution for the creditor's safety. When the Court of Chancery took notice of this practice, it became, and it still is, the established doctrine that such a deposit of deeds constitutes an "equitable mortgage" of itself. This doctrine being founded on the supposed equitableness of executing the agreement between the lender and borrower, and not on any virtue of the title-deeds in themselves, it does not matter whether the documents actually deposited are the whole of the debtor's evidence of title, and it even seems that it does not matter whether they are title-deeds at all, so long as they are stated so to be, and accepted as such by the creditor. A clever and unscrupulous borrower may thus deposit part of his title-deeds with one creditor, part with another, make an express agreement for security with a third (if he can lull the suspicion excited by the deeds not being forthcoming, a feat which, though not easy, has been performed with success), and execute a legal conveyance by way of mortgage to a fourth, while the value of the property on which they rely for payment is wholly insufficient to satisfy them all. The judicial adjustment of the conflicting claims thus created, and the determination of the order of preference to be given to the several creditors, demand the solution of most intricate legal problems. The Court of Chancery has manfully faced these difficulties, and, with the laudable intention of doing complete justice, has introduced various rules and distinctions which in their turn, being worked out in great detail, have led to unforeseen and sometimes unreasonable consequences. It may be doubted whether these refinements have not, on the whole, done more harm than good.

Endeavours have been made by Parliament at different times, from the end of the seventeenth century onwards, to deter borrowers on landed security from committing fraud on lenders by the concealment of earlier charges. These, however, have been but moderately successful, and the present state of things is anything but satisfactory. A lender may assure himself that there is at least one mortgage prior to his own, but he cannot be sure that there is only one, or any definite number.[1] Neither the Court of Chancery nor Parliament is much to blame. The power of encumbering land by secret and informal charges is but the natural outcome of the events which followed the Statute of Uses. When once the Statute of Enrolments was successfully evaded, and no fresh measure taken to restore the original purpose of the Statute of Uses, it was settled for many generations to come that dealings with land, instead of being, as the old law required, open and notorious,

[1] Cp. *Solicitors' Journal*, xxx. 208.

might be private and secret. The refinements and perplexities of "equitable mortgages" have only carried out this principle. And if the Legislature or the public are minded to have any effectual amendment, they must in turn consider whether there is any way short of wholly reversing the principles of modern conveyancing, and going back, in principle though not in form, to the ancient ways of the fathers of the Common Law.

CHAPTER VI

A LANDHOLDER whose land is more than he can occupy
and manage himself, and who does not choose to part
with the ownership, can use it in the following ways :—
He may, where slavery exists, cultivate the land by slave
labour under overseers. He may cause it to be cultivated, still at his own risk and for his own profit, by the
hired labour of freemen under the management of an
agent or bailiff. Or he may hand over the cultivation
and the profits to some person who makes his own
advantage of it on agreed terms and conditions, paying
for the use of the land either in money or by a share of
the produce. The first of these methods is not now
possible in any considerable part of the civilised world,
and has not existed in Europe at any time or place which
need be regarded for our purpose. The second is every-
where possible in law, and is common, I believe, on
some parts of the Continent, but in England a large
owner who farms his own land is now met with only as
an occasional exception. The third plan, namely, letting
the land to a tenant-farmer, has been, in one or another
form, generally adopted in modern times. Yet another,
which cannot be classed with any of these, was prevalent

in the Middle Ages; that is, the holders of small tenements were bound by custom to do agricultural work,
of stated amount and at stated seasons, on other land
possessed for his own use by the lord under whom they
held. These customary services may be called labour-
rents; they probably represented what we now call the
letting value of the land, but we must remember that
they were not dealt with as a matter of contract. As
often as not they were rendered by personally freemen;
in the case of a bondman's holding the services were
more burdensome and the tenure less assured, though
a comparison of the medieval text-writers with such
detailed records as are accessible suggests that by those
writers, and still more by the later ones who have built
upon their statements, the precariousness of even the
bondman's tenure is exaggerated. At least as early as
the thirteenth century these labour-dues were largely
commuted into fixed money payments. In the latter
half of the fourteenth century the depopulation and
scarcity of labour following on the Black Death went
far to break up the system, and by the beginning of
the sixteenth century money-rents appear to have fully
taken the place of personal service. The same causes
which made the old labour-rents worthless also made it
unprofitable to the landlord to farm his own land by
bailiffs, and thus the way was cleared for the modern
usage of letting to tenants.[1]

[1] Archdeacon Hale's Introduction to *Domesday of St. Paul's*, p.
lvi. Thorold Rogers's *History of Prices*. Vinogradoff, *Villainage
in England*. Much interesting and useful information on the social
aspects of the history of tenancy in England is also to be found in
Part I. of Mr. G. Brodrick's *English Land and English Landlords*.

Not that this usage is of modern origin. The beginning of it may be traced at least a century further back than the Norman Conquest. Religious foundations, the greatest owners of land in the earlier Middle Ages, and also the least able to give direct attention to its management, made temporary grants to tenants from an early time. Towards the end of the tenth century we find Oswald, Bishop of Worcester, explaining in a letter to King Edgar his practice of letting church lands to a tenant for three lives (the lives being the tenant's own, and those of two other persons named by him as successors) on the terms of rendering specified services; and several examples of these grants are preserved.[1] Two or three centuries later the practice of the Dean and Chapter of St. Paul's was to let their farms for life (sometimes to two tenants for the life of the survivor), the tenant rendering a fixed supply of provisions for the use of the house, with or without money payments in addition.[2] The farm buildings and live stock were found by the landlord, and the stock had to be accounted for at the end of the tenancy. The métayer system of farm-holding, still prevalent in many parts of the Continent, is not unlike this.

When tenancies for a fixed term of years came into use is not certain; they were well known, however, in the thirteenth century, and were common in the fifteenth. We may perhaps assume that letting for a certain term was suggested by the rotation of crops. A three years'

---

[1] *Cod. Dipl.* No. 1287, and Introd. vol. I. p. xxxiv. It does not appear whether the two succeeding lives must be those of persons in existence during the original tenant's life.

[2] *Domesday of St. Paul's,* xxxviii. 122 sqq.

lease, according to the old-fashioned husbandry, would
enable the tenant to complete the round and secure the
advantage of the wheat crop ; and a term of three years
is in fact the shortest that occurs in practice. Yearly
tenancy, now the commonest form of holding in England,
is not a letting for one year, but "from year to year,"
that is, for an indefinite time, determinable by either
party giving notice (formerly a half-year's notice, but
now a whole year's in the absence of agreement to the
contrary) [1] at the proper season. Perpetual leases, after
the fashion of the Roman emphyteusis, are unknown to
English law, but there is no legal limit to the certain
number of years for which a lease may be granted, and
therefore no technical difficulty in the way of making it
as good as perpetual. In practice twenty-one years is
the greatest length of agricultural and occupation leases.[2]
Building leases are commonly made for ninety-nine years
(but of late often for not more than eighty), and mining
leases (which, as being in truth a sale of the minerals
to be worked by the lessee, are in sundry ways peculiar)
for terms varying with local usage, not as a rule exceeding sixty years. Longer terms, as of 200, 500, or
even 1000 years, are conferred upon trustees as part of
the machinery of family settlements, and were for some
time commonly used in mortgages ; it is enough here, if
it be not too much, to mention their existence. In these
cases there is no rent and no real tenancy. Leases for

[1] Agricultural Holdings (England) Act, 1883, s. 33.
[2] In many American States the length of farming leases is re-
stricted by statute to ten or twelve years. On the other hand, a
lease for a term of years with a covenant for perpetual renewal is a
common form of urban tenure.

lives, renewable by custom on payment of a fine as often
as a life fell in, were until lately the common method of
managing ecclesiastical and corporate lands. The object
of adopting this plan was simply to benefit the existing
bishop or corporators at the expense of the see, college,
or other corporate body, the fines, as they were received
for successive renewals, being treated not as capital,
which they really were, but as revenue. Modern reforms
have put an end to this, I believe, in every case.

Leaving exceptional cases aside, we pass on to consider the position of the tenant who holds either for a
term of years, or as tenant from year to year. In the
feudal plan of society there is no place for him; and
accordingly the legal doctrine starts from the conception
that the relation between the landlord and the tenant
is simply a personal contract. This conception is at the
bottom of all the differences between freehold and leasehold tenure, and, though largely qualified in its effects,
must be borne in mind in order to understand even the
most modern form of the law. The lessee's interest is
now beyond question property, not the mere right to
the performance of a contract. Still, being in legal
theory the creature of contract, it has neither the dig-
nities nor the burdens peculiar to freehold tenures.
It is not the subject of feudal modes of conveyance, nor
of the feudal rules of inheritance. No particular form
of words is necessary for its creation; and the custom of
creating it by deed has become a legal requirement (and
that not in every case) only by modern statutes. It
could always be disposed of by will if the tenant died
before the expiration of the term; and in case of such
death the law deals with it in the same way as cattle or

money, and it goes to the executor, as part of the "personal estate," to be administered by the same rules as movable property. If undisposed of by will, the leasehold tenant's interest belongs on his death to the same persons, and in the same proportions, as cash or railway shares which he has not disposed of. There is no such thing as an heir of leaseholds. In one word, which for the lawyer includes all that has been said, a leasehold is not *real* but *personal* estate. From a strictly feudal point of view there is not an estate at all, only a personal claim against the freeholder to be allowed to occupy the land in accordance with the agreement. But as early as the thirteenth century two points were settled, which together constituted a true right of property in the tenant. If he was ejected in breach of his landlord's agreement, he could recover not merely compensation for being turned out, but the possession itself; and this not only against the original landlord, but against a purchaser from him. Already the purchaser could not say to the tenant whom he found on the land, "I have made no contract with you; look for your redress to the man with whom you did contract." The farmer's possession was as secure while his estate lasted as the freeholder's.[1] On the foundation thus laid the modern law has been completed, partly by judicial usage and partly by express legislation. Broadly speaking, both the landlord's and the tenant's successors in title enjoy, while the term of the tenancy lasts, the

---

[1] "Non magis poterit aliquis firmarium eiicere de firma sua quam tenentem aliquem de libero tenemento suo."—Bracton, fo. 220*b*. For details see the section on "The Term of Years," in Pollock and Maitland, *Hist. Eng. Law*, ii. 105-17.

rights conferred at its creation upon the landlord and tenant respectively, and are subject to the burdens imposed on them. Exceptions may still occur, too rare and technical to be now further specified, which are just enough to show that the old notion of a more personal agreement, though decayed, is not dead.

There is, however, one ancient and peculiar incident in the relation between landlord and tenant which the theory of contract is incapable of explaining. This is the landlord's right of distress. Early records, both of English customs and of those of kindred nations, point to a time when distress was almost the universal form of civil remedy. When cattle were the only movable property of any value, and courts of justice had no swift or certain means of enforcing their orders, the most natural thing for a man to do who complained of wrong at his neighbour's hands was to drive off some of the neighbour's cattle, and keep them till the owner would either satisfy his claim or refer the matter to the decision of an impartial authority. Still more obvious is the form of self-help, preserved in our law to this day, which is called "distraint damage feasant"; that is, impounding cattle [1] which trespass upon one's land as a security that the damage shall be made good. When courts of justice began to compel the attendance of parties before them (for there are traces everywhere of a time when they professed only to do justice between such as willingly submitted themselves), they applied the same kind of compulsion that was in familiar use in private quarrels.

[1] Goods of any kind may be distrained damage feasant, and a locomotive has been so dealt with by a railway company; but animals only need to be regarded for the present purpose.

As local jurisdiction passed into the hands of lords of
manors, distress became the regular means of compelling
persons subject to the lord's jurisdiction to appear in his
court, and also, with or without judicial proceedings in
the court, of enforcing payment or performance of the
rents and services due from tenants.   Some local customs
even allowed the lord to seize the land itself.   By steps
of which nothing certain is known, it came to be understood that an agreement for the occupancy of land, though
it created no feudal tenure, and therefore no service in
the proper sense, entitled the owner, if the rent fell into
arrear, to seize any goods he could find on the land as a
security for its payment.   Probably the right was claimed
and exercised without dispute by analogy to the rights
of the lord of a manor against his freehold tenants.   It
may have contributed to the readier allowance, as it
certainly does to the apparent justice of the proceeding,
that in the Middle Ages the live stock of the farm were
mostly supplied by the landlord.   In such a case, if the
tenant became insolvent, a landlord who seized the
stock was only resuming his own.   Be the early history
what it may, the right has existed ever since English
common law took a definite shape.[1]   In the course of
the last two centuries legislation has made it a far
more efficient instrument in favour of the landlord ;

---

[1] The student may consult, besides Sir H. Maine's chapter on
the Primitive Forms of Legal Remedies, the chapter on Distraint
in Mr. Bigelow's *History of Procedure in England*.   For the common law in its settled form, see Blackstone, book iii. ch. i.   Our
early medieval law was in general stricter against self-help than
the modern law ; see Pollock and Maitland, *Hist. Eng. Law*, ii. 573.
Nevertheless the landlord's right of distress without judgment grew
up apparently without dispute.

which has indeed been the tendency of all legislation concerning landlords and tenants until a pretty recent time.

By the common law things taken in distress were a mere pledge for payment of the rent. Therefore nothing might be distrained which could not be restored in the same condition, such as corn in sheaves; nor anything which grew out of or was fixed to the soil, such as standing corn; and the landlord had no power to sell distrained beasts or goods, nor to deal with them in any way as owner, even for the owner's benefit, except, perhaps, in case of evident necessity.[1] And, moreover, as Blackstone tells us, "the many particulars which attend the taking of a distress used formerly to make it a hazardous kind of proceeding; for, if any one irregularity was committed, it vitiated the whole," and the person distraining became a mere trespasser. This has already been noticed by Sir Henry Maine as evidence of the archaic nature of the institution. "The excessive technicality of ancient law" clings to all ancient customary remedies unless and until, as in this case, modern legislators remove it for the benefit of the parties, or one of them. In 1689 the power of selling things taken by distress, after notice to the tenant, was first given to the landlord by Act of Parliament; it was further secured and defined by subsequent statutes of

---

[1] It has been said that he had no right to milk a cow. The learned reader may compare the somewhat similar proposition that milking the testator's cow will make a man executor de son tort. But the statement is only in Rolle's Abridgement, L. 673, and is directly contradicted by the report of the same case in Cro. Jac. 147, where things done of necessity and for the owner's benefit are excepted from the general rule.

the eighteenth century, and the old restrictions on the kinds of things liable to distress were greatly relaxed. "The summary power of sale now exercised has been created by the recent statute law with more attention to the profit of the rich than to the rights which were secured to the poor by our ancient jurisprudence." [1]

It will be understood that the right of the landlord is other and greater than the tenant could give him by contract: it is to take chattels found on the holding, whether the tenant's property or not. This, if it were simply a matter of agreement, the tenant could of course not enable the landlord to do: contracts cannot impose liabilities on persons who are not parties. In the case of under-tenancies, a thing unknown when the rule of law was fixed, great hardship may be the result, since the goods of a sub-tenant may be distrained for rent due from his immediate lessor to the superior landlord. This "great loss and injustice" (in the words adopted by Parliament) was remedied in the case of lodgers by an Act passed as lately as 1871. The expediency of the right of distress as regards farm holdings has in recent years been much discussed. It is rational to say that, since the landlord cannot help giving credit, he ought to be in some shape and to some extent a preferred creditor: but the existing law of distress gives effect to this principle in the most rough and irrational fashion. It would seem that the advocates of complete "freedom of contract" in the relations between landlord and tenant ought to have been the first to demand the abolition of an anomalous customary privilege which contract could never have been engendered; but such was by no means

[1] Palgrave, *English Commonwealth*, i. 182.

the case. By the Agricultural Holdings Act of 1883 (46 & 47 Vict. c. 61) the landlord's right to distrain, which at common law extended to six years' back rent, is limited to one year as regards holdings within the Act—that is, farm, pasture, and market-garden lands: and hired machinery, and live stock not being the tenant's own property, are exempt from distress—the former absolutely, the latter with certain qualifications.

It may be regarded as a kind of set-off to the power of distress that other summary powers and remedies which lessors are in the habit of securing to themselves by contract have lately been mitigated in their operation, so as to prevent them from being abused beyond their true function of securing the landlord's interest. For a long time it has been the common practice to insert in leases, especially of town property, provisions enabling the landlord to re-enter and put an end to the lease if the tenant fails to perform his obligations. Non-payment of rent is the cause most commonly specified; another is neglect to keep the premises insured, where the tenant has covenanted to insure; frequently the clause of re-entry extends to breach or neglect of any one of the tenant's covenants.[1] With regard to non-payment of rent, the tenant became entitled, first by the practice of the Court of Chancery, and then by modern Acts of Parliament, to be relieved from forfeiting the lease on payment of the rent in arrear and costs. About twenty years ago neglect to insure was also made remissible on certain conditions. And now by the Conveyancing Act of 1881 (sec. 14)

[1] Covenant, which etymologically is a mere synonym of agreement, signifies in English law any promise made by deed.

the Court has power to grant relief to the tenant in its discretion, and on such terms as it thinks fit, except in the case of non-payment of rent, as to which the former Acts remain in force.

Another general rule of law which bore hardly on tenants has gradually been relaxed in their favour, namely, that which declares that things affixed to the soil become for legal purposes part of it, and cease to be the tenant's. The truth is, and it may as well be stated at this point, that the law of landlord and tenant has never, at least under any usual conditions, been a law of free contract. It is a law of contract partly express, partly supplied by judicial interpretation, and partly controlled by legislation and sometimes by local custom. So far as the terms and conditions are express, they are in the vast majority of cases framed by landlords or their advisers. The tendency of judicial interpretation has also been, until lately, to incline the scale of presumption in favour of the landlord on doubtful points; and the same may be said of the ruling tendency of legislation down to the middle of the present century. The allowance of local customs, which might have done much to redress the balance if taken up betimes, depends on the tendency of the judges. When special customs were looked on as a kind of natural enemies of the common law, and strict proof of them was required, they got little help in court. Probably many tenants have in past times failed to establish customary rights, or have been discouraged by the failure of others from asserting them, in cases where the decision would now be the other way.[1] As

[1] A good example of the present tendency to give full effect to

to the point now in hand, it was settled early in the eighteenth century that a tenant might at any time before the end of his term remove fixtures set up by him for purposes of trade. Early in the present century the judges, with unfortunate timidity, declined to extend the same principle to buildings and fixtures provided by a tenant-farmer for purely agricultural use. What they did not see their way to declaring as common law has by successive steps been enacted by Parliament. By an Act of 1851 a tenant who, with the landlord's consent in writing, put up farm buildings or machinery at his own cost, was enabled to remove them as his own property, subject to an option on the landlord's part to take them at a valuation. The Agricultural Holdings Act of 1875 extended this right of the tenant (with some small variations of language in his favour) to engines, machinery, and fixtures affixed to the holding even without the landlord's consent, saving, however, to the landlord a right to object to the erection of a steam-engine: lastly, the Agricultural Holdings (England) Act, 1883, has re-enacted this provision without the saving.[1]

There remains a serious economical question between landlords and tenants, for which the common law failed to provide a solution. No general rule of law gives an outgoing tenant any compensation for permanent or unexhausted improvements made by him. A tenant who has a pretty long lease may no doubt so order matters as to get the full benefit of his improvements;

established local usage is afforded by the case of Tucker v. Linger, decided by the House of Lords in 1883, Law Rep. 8 App. Ca. 508.
[1] S. 34.

though even so it is the worse for the land to make it
the tenant's interest to leave nothing in it. But in
England yearly tenancy is the rule, and leases for fixed
terms the exception. In some parts of the country
local customs exist which have been found fairly satisfactory, providing a scale of compensation for the
tenant's outlay on lime, artificial manures, artificial
feeding stuffs, and the like. But these are of limited
extent, and applicable, as a rule, only to the soils and
agricultural usages of the particular districts where they
prevail.

After much discussion, and an experiment by way
of permissive legislation in 1875, on which it is no
longer necessary to dwell, the matter was dealt with
by the Agricultural Holdings Act of 1883. This Act
is somewhat clumsy in form, and bears in every part,
after the manner of all English legislation involving
a conflict of interests, the marks of compromise and
abundant caution. It has established, however, in
opposition to the old common law, the leading principle
that an outgoing tenant who has improved the holding
is entitled to get by way of compensation "such sum
as fairly represents the value of the improvement to an
incoming tenant." The improvements for which compensation may be obtained are, it is true, defined and
classified with excessive minuteness; and the previous
consent of the landlord to permanent improvements
(such as building, irrigation, planting, and reclaiming)
is a necessary condition of their being a subject of
compensation. As to this class of improvements,
therefore, the only effects of the Act are to make the
landlord's consent, if given, binding on the land and on

his successors (which, however, is important, having
regard to the great amount of land in settlement, or in
the hands of trustees or public bodies or officers with
limited powers), and to throw on the landlord the
burden and odium of refusing consent where the improvement is clearly a proper one.   Perhaps it was
impossible to go further consistently with the fundamental assumption of English leasehold tenure, that the
lessor is entitled to have back his land at the end of
the term in the same condition in which the lessee took
it.   As to drainage, a middle course is observed : the
tenant need not obtain the landlord's consent for drain-
ing the land, but he must give him notice of the intended work, and then the landlord may do it himself
if he thinks fit, and charge the tenant with an addition
to his rent by way of interest.   Exhaustible improvements, such as liming and manuring, may be made, and
will entitle the tenant to compensation, without the
landlord's consent.   Claims for compensation are to be
settled by reference ; the local county court may appoint a referee or umpire, as the case may require, in
default of either of the parties or their referees acting,
or either party may call for the nomination of an
umpire by the Board of Agriculture.   The Act contains,
moreover, a number of minor provisions and safeguards
for which the text itself must be consulted.[1]   It seems,
on the whole, fitted to carry out its objects with as
little friction and waste of power as, our system of

[1] There are some later amendments and extensions of the Act :
see the Tenants' Compensation Act, 1890, and the Market Gardeners'
Compensation Act, 1895. Similar but distinct provisions were
made for tenants of allotments by the Allotments and Cottage
Gardens Compensation for Crops Act, 1887.

legislation being what it is, can fairly be expected. But it remains a misfortune that the principle of compensation declared by the Act was not in the first instance adopted by the common law. Local usage and a certain amount of judicial decision would then have settled the method and details of the tenant's compensation much better than the clauses and schedules of a modern Act of Parliament can do it. We are no longer able to declare a broad principle and leave it to work itself out; we expect every question of detail to be met beforehand, and entangle ourselves in intolerable minuteness without, after all, being secure against material oversights. And we shall hardly escape or mitigate this evil until either we greatly extend the modern device of delegating legislative powers, or in some way return to the older fashion of legislating by way of general instructions and conferring a large discretion on the executive authority. This, however, belongs to the problems of the general theory of legislation.

Except as regards the special legislation for agricultural tenancies which has just been noticed, and which dates only from the middle of the present century, there is no difference in law between urban and agricultural leaseholds. But in practice and custom the difference is very great. Farm holdings are always or almost always taken by the tenant direct from the freeholder, and there is generally something of a personal relation between them (even where the landlord is a college or other corporate body) beyond the mere receipt and payment of rent. The farmer is legally bound to pay the full amount of his agreed rent, without regard to the goodness or badness of the season; but in bad years it is the constant practice for the landlord to remit such a percentage of the rent as to leave the tenant answerable only for so much as the farm seems fairly capable of paying under the circumstances. A great landlord who refused to follow this practice would be entirely within his legal rights, but would certainly be thought the worse of in the country. In many counties, unfortunately, reductions of 15 or 20 per cent (sometimes even more) have now been rather the rule than the exception for some years past. The landlord in return expects a certain amount of deference and compliance in various matters from his tenant. Not only does the farmer meet him half-way on questions of shooting rights, and allow free passage to the hunt, but his political support of the landlord is not unfrequently reckoned on with as much confidence as the performance of the covenants and conditions of the tenancy itself. In the case of holdings from year to year it may be not unfairly said that being of the landlord's political party is often a tacit condition of the tenancy.

In the letting of buildings for occupation, whether for business or as dwelling-houses, and especially in large towns, there is nothing of this kind. The transaction and the relations of the parties are purely a matter of commerce. The owner of land on which there stands a shop or a factory sells the right to occupy it to the shopkeeper or manufacturer just as he in turn sells his goods, that is, for the highest price he can get. And the same rule holds as to leases of mines and collieries, where the sale is not merely of the right to use the land, but of a portion of the land itself, namely, the coal, ores, or other minerals to be worked by the lessee.   As regards occupation leases, again, underletting, instead of being the exception, is the rule in the south of England.   The freeholder of building land in or near a town makes a lease of it to a builder for a term, which used to be of ninety-nine years, but is now (at least in and about London) commonly not more than eighty.   The builder undertakes to cover the ground with a house or number of houses, according to requirements laid down by the landlord in more or less detail.   At the end of the term the buildings become the landlord's property, the lessee finding his compensation in such profit as he can make of them during the term by subletting to occupying tenants.   In houses of a good class, which are occupied as a whole, there is commonly only one underletting.   But there may be more ; and in the case of smaller tenements the actual dweller often has to pay several intermediate profits, getting in return bad quarters and a precarious tenure. The system of building leases is convenient for the freeholder, as it saves him all trouble beyond that of laying out the plan or the general character of the buildings to be put on the land, and ensures him the possession of his property greatly increased in value at the end of the term.   He might build himself and let direct to occupiers, thus getting the full profit at once, but he would then incur also the trouble and risk which by the usual arrangement are thrown on the first lessee, commonly known as the "speculative builder."   For all other parties, and it would seem for the public, the plan is a thoroughly bad one.   As the builder has no

permanent interest in his work, he has no motive for
making it durable, and is tempted to make it, on the
contrary, as bad as the ground landlord's surveyor can
be induced to pass, and occupying tenants to accept for
their habitation. He buys the use of the land from
the freeholder for a limited time, and retails it to the
public either directly or through a middleman. All
the risks of the retail market fall on him; some time
must elapse at best before he can make a profit, for it
takes time, even with hurried and flimsy work, to
build houses and make them look fit to live in. There
is no business in which profits are more uncertain, and
none, I believe, in which there is more insolvency; on
the other hand, great fortunes have been made by well-
known builders in London and elsewhere. When the
builder's or middleman's turn comes, it is of course
his interest to make the most he can out of the under-
tenant for the time allowed him. Dwelling-houses,
therefore, are necessarily rack-rented.[1] By well-to-do
sorts of people this is perhaps not felt as a grave inconvenience, but the pressure and hardship on the smaller
under-tenants are very great.

It is evidently absurd to speak of freedom of contract in relation to such a system. Desirable building
ground near towns, and still more the ground of towns
and cities already long occupied, and eminently those
districts and sites which are favoured by business or
fashion, are a monopoly in the hands of the landowner.

[1] Rack-rent, I need hardly explain, is the highest annual rent
that can be obtained by the competition of those who desire to
become tenants. It is not a strictly legal term, though sometimes
used in Acts of Parliament; in legal documents it is represented
by "the best rent that can be obtained without a fine."

The landowner dictates his terms to the building lessee, who in turn dictates them to the occupier, making the occupier's obligations, for his own protection, exactly follow those of the original lease. In this way the population of whole cities may be said to live at the will of a few great landlords. Over whole square miles of what is commonly called London the Duke of Westminster or the Duke of Bedford may without appeal or control forbid any given kind of building to exist, or any given kind of business to be carried on. In the eye of the law the Westminster, or Bedford, or Portman estate is simply so much land in the administrative county of London, which the freeholder need not have built upon, or allowed others to build upon, unless he chose. If he does not choose to sell, and chooses to grant building leases, it is for people to take or leave, —as, where it is difficult to find a tenant for a farm in depressed times, it may be for the landlord to take or leave the tenant. Accidents of site and social conditions may give the freeholder a supreme monopoly, but that is his good fortune, an extraneous matter with which the law does not concern itself. That such powers are used, on the whole, with so little ground for complaint as they are, is much to the credit of human nature and of the training of English gentlemen. But the matter involves more than one serious problem for the next generation, if not for our own. The value of land for occupation in towns has increased out of all proportion to the increase in the value of other land ; it is comparatively little affected by the depression of agricultural industry, and no reason appears why the increase should not continue. This affords another

potent reason why the fortunate owners of city ground-
rents should go on leasing rather than selling; for to
sell the freehold of such ground as the bounds of the
city of London encompass is to part—however great be
the price in hand—with potential riches beyond all
present valuation. We are in sight of an accumulation
of wealth and power in a few hands, and concentrated
on vital parts of the commonwealth, such as is without
example in history, and might conceivably be a danger
to the State. But it is far more easy to perceive the
danger than to devise a remedy. In Scotland the
practice is to grant the land in perpetuity for a fixed
rent (which under the feudal rules of Scottish law is
easily done by a form of conveyance called in modern
practice a "feu-contract"); building leases of the English type are, I believe, unknown. In the north of
England it is not uncommon to do what comes nearly
to the same thing in a less direct form by conveying
the land in fee-simple and taking an annual payment
out of it under the name of rent-charge.[1] But this is
anything but satisfactory, for every part of the land is
liable for the whole rent: therefore, if the subject-
matter of the original grant is subdivided among other
purchasers (which constantly happens), the occupying
owner will find himself under liabilities which are uncertain and in possible events may be ruinous. Leases
for a very long term, such as 999 years, have sometimes
been used for the same object, and are open to the same

---

[1] Since the statute of *Quia emptores* (p. 70 above) a rent proper
cannot be reserved upon a grant in fee-simple except by the Crown.
There was never any corresponding enactment in practical force in
Scotland, and the statute is not in force in some American States.

inconvenience. In other parts of the north country the land is sold off in plots to builders who become absolute owners; the simplest plan of all, and, if the parties will use it, the most rational.

It has been proposed to confer on lessees of house and cottage property the power of acquiring the freehold by way of compulsory purchase, or, to put it in a neater and perhaps more easily understood form, to attach a statutory option of purchase to all leases of a certain length. The terms would have to be in each case settled either by arbitration or by some kind of judicial process if the parties could not agree; the reference clauses of the Agricultural Holdings Act might serve for the first lines of a working plan. The first effect of such a law would probably be to check the supply of building land and dwelling-houses by making landowners unwilling to grant new leases, and thus to aggravate for the time the evils of monopoly. What would be the ulterior effects it is not easy to foretell. It seems doubtful whether the acquisition of permanent interests by the people most in want of them would really be much facilitated. And it does not seem clear that building lessees are now, as a rule, anxious to acquire the freehold: for if they were so, they could and would find opportunities even under the present system. Urban freeholders are not often willing to sell, but forced sales are every now and then brought about by various causes. Still, it is something to recognise that a problem has to be faced. The idea of "leasehold enfranchisement" has at least such elements of a solution as to deserve consideration, and in London and one or two parts of the country it has attracted

serious attention. In 1886 a Select Committee of the
House of Commons was appointed to consider questions
connected with town holdings; it finally reported
on leasehold enfranchisement in 1889.[1] The report
allowed that some advantages were likely to attend the
conversion of leasehold into freehold tenure, but recommended only the partial application of the principle
through powers to be given to local authorities over
limited areas. Nothing has been done to give effect to
this report. In later years there has been less heard
of local enfranchisement and more of "betterment"
and the taxation of ground-rent; but the intricate controversy which has beset the last-mentioned topics is
beyond the scope of this work.

It seems fit to be weighed whether any systematic
reform of urban tenure should not aim at making
the municipalities rather than individual occupiers the
ultimate owners. One or two of our northern cities,
by using such occasions as presented themselves from
time to time of acquiring property within their own
borders, have already made some way in this direction.
The recent Allotments Act, of which some account
must now be given, is in the same direction so far as
it goes.

Good landlords have long been in the habit of en-
couraging labourers dwelling on their estates to become
tenants of small allotments, and cultivate them for
their own profit and pleasure in spare time. But it
has appeared that individual goodwill and enlighten-
ment cannot always be trusted to make reasonable

---

[1] Parl. P. 1889, xv. 1. On the ground-rent question there is a
further report of 1892.

provision of this kind; and Parliament has now conferred on local authorities a limited power of acquiring
land for allotments if satisfied that adequate voluntary
arrangements cannot be made. The Allotments Act,
1887, 50 & 51 Vict. c. 48, enables the local sanitary
authority, being so satisfied, to buy or hire suitable
land, by agreement if possible; failing agreement, the
County Council may, on petition from the sanitary
authority, making a provisional order conferring powers
of compulsory purchase similar to those exercised by
railway companies and other public bodies for other
purposes of public interest. The provisional order
must be confirmed by Act of Parliament in order to
become effective. Parks, gardens, and the private
grounds of dwelling-houses are absolutely excepted
from compulsory taking. Allotment land acquired
under the Act is to be so let and managed as to make
the undertaking self-supporting. Allotments are not
to exceed one acre, and sub-letting is forbidden. It
will be seen that the Act rather holds out a distant
prospect of compulsion than attempts any direct interference with private discretion. It was intended to
operate as a gentle stimulus to landowners to follow,
where practicable and not yet practised, the example
already set by the best of them; and in this way it
has done considerable good. Sometimes, I believe not
often, the compulsory powers have been exercised.

By the Small Holdings Act, 1892, local authorities
are empowered to acquire land in their own names
and sell or let it in small parcels for agricultural
occupation; and under the Local Government Act, 1894,
parish councils have power (which may be made com-

pulsory by an order of the County Council, on proper cause being shown) to hire land for allotments. It would be useless to give details here.[1]

[1] Information as to the working of the Allotments and Small Holdings Acts can easily be obtained from the publications of the Rural Labourers' League (96 Colmore Row, Birmingham).

CHAPTER VII

For about a century and a half there was no material change in the English law of real property. There was, indeed, in the early part of the eighteenth century a period of minor reforms, which are at this day perhaps not sufficiently remembered. The mechanism of judicial and other proceedings was in some respects simplified, and some opportunities of fraud still afforded by obsolete doctrines were removed. But the work of the preceding century was in the main left untouched. The statute which abolished the military tenures marks the end of one period of transformation. The Act for the Abolition of Fines and Recoveries passed by the first reformed Parliament marks the beginning of another which is still in progress. As a help to memory, the Restoration and the Reform Act of 1832 may well be thus taken as the landmarks, although the current form of settlement of landed property was not fully worked out until towards the middle of the eighteenth century, and on the other hand the movement leading to the series of legal reforms now to be spoken of was formally begun, by the appointment of a commission of inquiry, some years before it bore fruit, and was in substance due in great measure to the labours of Bentham. And Bentham's criticism was in turn provoked and made possible by Black-stone's artistic exposition of the settled form of the law which in his own time was still recent. So it is every-where, both in nature and in the affairs of man; what seems to be repose is in truth the preparation of change.

It will be convenient to take the modern alterations of the law not in order of time, which would lead to great intricacy and to the confusion of distinct topics, but according to the subject-matter. And first we will take the formal simplification of dealings with land. From the latter part of the sixteenth century onwards the common mode of conveying freehold land, as we have seen, was by the ingeniously artificial process of "lease and release" (p. 106 above), which involved the bulk and expense of two deeds. The length of these documents also steadily increased until about the begin-ning of the present century; partly by reason of the greater complication of the affairs and interests to be dealt with, and the new precautions devised by lawyers to meet newly-discovered dangers to titles, partly because, by an evil usage which has only in the last few years been abated, professional skill was recompensed merely in proportion to the amount of writing produced. In 1845 (after one or two rather clumsy experiments, which it is needless to specify) the first of these troubles was removed in a manner so simple and elegant as to com-mand the approval of even the conservative school of conveyancers. The ceremony of feoffment was always in-applicable to an estate in reversion or remainder. Livery of seisin—the formal transfer of possession which has been described elsewhere (p. 75 above)—could be given

only by one who had the actual possession to one who
had it not. A freeholder not having the right of actual
possession (as where the land was held by a tenant for
life or a lessee) disposed of his interest by deed without
other ceremony; it was an "incorporeal hereditament"
which could not be delivered. The same rule applied to
such rights over the lands of others, rent-charges, rights
of way or common, and the like, as were capable of disposition and transfer. All rights and interests that could
be so dealt with were said to "lie in grant." The Act to
amend the Law of Real Property passed in 1845 extended this rule to estates in possession.[1] Since it took
effect everything which can be done by feoffment, bargain
and sale enrolled, or lease and release, can be equally well
done by a simple deed; and although the older forms of
conveyance are still open to any one who might choose to
make use of them, the readier way provided by this Act
has been almost universally followed. Certain further
simplifications as to the use of particular words (not all
of them really new) have been introduced by the Conveyancing Act of 1881. They are too technical to be
dwelt on here; only it is worth notice that they do not
touch the substance of the old feudal rule—namely, that
a grant to a man without specifying what interest he is
to have will give him no more than an estate for life.[2]

---

[1] "After the said first day of October, one thousand eight
hundred and forty-five, all corporeal tenements shall, as regards
the conveyance of the immediate freehold thereof, be deemed to
lie in grant as well as in livery."—8 & 9 Vict. c. 106, s. 6. The
capacity which a feoffment formerly had of practically giving a
purchaser a better title than his vendor's (p. 82 above) was abolished
by the same statute.

[2] 44 & 45 Vict. c. 41, s. 49, etc. These provisions have already

As to the other point of the prolixity of deeds, much more was left for the Conveyancing Act to do. In the same year (1845), and I suppose under the same auspices as the Act to amend the Law of Real Property, a statute was made with the laudable intention of substituting short forms for the accustomed verbose ones. It was a complete failure, partly from defects of workmanship which made it positively misleading, but chiefly because no legal practitioner who adopted it would, under the vicious scheme of remuneration then in use, have been tolerably paid for his work. The abbreviated forms provided by the statute were seldom or never used, and for another generation deeds went on being framed as before, though the practice of the best conveyancers was now to study conciseness. At last in 1881 a new Act ("The Conveyancing and Law of Property Act, 1881 ") dealt with the form of deeds relating to land in a far more thorough-going and elaborate manner. The use of a few prescribed words will now incorporate in a deed, according to the nature of the case, one or other of the several accustomed clauses which were formerly inserted at full length ; and in ordinary straightforward cases this may conveniently and safely be done. At the same time another Act (the Solicitors' Remuneration Act) abolished the necessity or supposed necessity of paying for the preparation of deeds according to length, and thus left the way clear for the Conveyancing Act. This last, however, is not compulsory ; people may go on using the old forms as much as they please, but the

given rise, I believe, to a popular error that the use of the word *grant* is not only unnecessary but improper, whereas it remains as proper as ever.

new provisions have been generally adopted. Supplementary Acts were passed in 1882, and (for the further protection of lessees) in 1892, but the points dealt with (as well as many of those covered by the Act of 1881) are too technical to be specified in this work. The credit of these measures belongs to both parties in the State; they were substantially prepared under the direction of Lord Cairns in the later years of the Conservative Ministry which held office from 1874 to 1880, and were taken up and passed into law with little alteration by the Liberal Ministry which succeeded. The same may be said concerning the Settled Land Act, of which we have to speak later.

The cumbrous machinery of fines and common recoveries (which has been described in Chapter IV.) was swept away in 1833, and a tenant in tail is now empowered, by means of a deed enrolled in Chancery, to make either himself, or any one to whom he wishes to dispose of his estate, a tenant in fee simple. If he is in possession of the freehold, he can generally do this without any other person's consent. If he is not in possession, he must, as a rule, have the consent of the "protector of the settlement," who is commonly the tenant for life, otherwise he can create no greater estate than a *base fee* (p. 113 above). The name and function of the "protector" were introduced by the Act of 1833; but the purpose and the effect of the Act were, while simplifying the necessary proceedings, to preserve intact in substance the law and practice of family settlements. Considered as an improvement in form, which is all it professed to be, the Act for the Abolition of Fines and Recoveries has been of great

service, and has worked with singular freedom from
difficulties of any kind.   This success is due in some
measure to the circumstance (not so common, unhappily,
that notice of it should be superfluous) that the framing
of the Act was entrusted to a man who thoroughly
understood the matter he was to deal with.

It seems worth while to quote a few sentences from
the First Report of the Real Property Commissioners to
show how the problems of law reform presented themselves two generations ago to learned and enlightened
persons.   It will be seen that the limitation of their
proposals was the result not of opposition or compromise
but of free and deliberate conviction.

"The owner of the soil is, we think, vested with
exactly the dominion and power of disposition over it
required for the public good, and landed property in
England is admirably made to answer all the purposes
to which it is applicable.

"Settlements bestow on the present possessor of an
estate the benefits of ownership, and secure the property
to his posterity.   The existing rule respecting perpetuities has happily hit the medium between the strict
entails which prevail in the northern part of the Island,[1]
and by which the property entailed is for ever abstracted
from commerce, and the total prohibition of substitutions
and the excessive restriction of the power of devising
established in some countries on the Continent of
Europe.[2]   In England families are preserved, and pur-

[1] It was then possible to create inviolable entails in Scotland ;
the law has since been changed, and alienation is as easy as in
England.

[2] Meaning probably those which adopted or imitated the Code
Napoléon.

chasers always find a supply of land in the market. A testamentary power is given, which stimulates industry and encourages accumulation; and while capricious limitations are restrained, property is allowed to be moulded according to the circumstances and wants of every family."

Thus the Commissioners in 1829.[1] Lord St. Leonards would have been in their eyes a rash innovator, Lord Cairns a revolutionist, and for Lord Halsbury parliamentary language would have failed them. But we are anticipating.

Another point where simplification was urgently called for, and was carried out a few years later, was the disposal of land (as well as of other property) by will. The state of things before 1838 (brought about by steps which we need not consider) was that the formalities required for a will of lands were excessive, those for a will of leaseholds or movables absurdly and dangerously defective. There were also peculiar rules and exceptions (partly by common law, partly by custom, and partly by statute) in particular cases, and, on the whole, it was found on careful inquiry that there were ten different laws for regulating the execution of wills under different circumstances.[2] An Act of 1837, which applies to all wills made since the end of that year, abolished all these intricacies, together with many other inconveniences and doubts, and established the uniform rule that a will must be signed by the maker of it, and attested by two witnesses. It also applied to wills the rule— still not applicable to deeds—that a simple and unquali-

---

[1] First Report, p. 6.
[2] Fourth Report of Real Property Commissioners, p. 12.

fied gift is to be taken as disposing of the giver's whole interest.

It is not the length of deeds, however, nor any formality required for either deeds or wills, that is the real source of expense and trouble in dealing with English land. The peculiar system of private conveyance which has grown up under the shadow of the Statute of Uses has made it needful for purchasers to secure themselves against the "constant danger from secret transfers and secret charges"[1] by an examination of the history of the property as evidenced by the title-deeds. Except in the rare cases where estates have been settled by Act of Parliament, and in the case of land registered under the Land Registry Act of 1875, undisturbed possession under a continuous title for a certain length of time is the only proof of the rightful ownership of land in this country. The title-deeds are the written history of the possession, and of the right in which it has been exercised; and from this point of view their contents are, or in strict prudence ought to be, examined by every purchaser. Almost always this operation requires some professional skill; often it requires much. In all but the simplest cases the process is a long and costly one. Not only solicitors and counsel have to be paid for their intellectual work, but a good deal of clerical and mechanical labour is involved in making and verifying copies or abstracts,[2] searching certain official records

[1] First Report of Real Property Commissioners, p. 8.

[2] The digest of documents and facts laid before counsel as the basis of his opinion is called an "abstract of title." It is the solicitor's business to verify the contents of this, the counsel's to point out, if necessary, what further verification is required, and to advise whether, assuming the statements to be correct, they

which might disclose matters affecting the title, and the
like. All this falls on the buyer, and in the case of
small properties acts as an exorbitant tax added to the
purchase-money ; for the cost and difficulties are no less
for a small property than for a large one. Indeed large
properties are better off ; for there are some estates of
which the possession and title are historical, and so well
known that, if a portion is to be sold or let, the owners
can afford to make what terms they please as to dispens-
ing with inquiry. Less fortunate sellers have to examine
their own titles before going into the market, and to
guard themselves against requisitions which it might be
impossible or ruinous to comply with by selling only on
carefully framed special terms, which are known, if the
sale is by auction, as "conditions of sale." Very few
landowners are in a position to make out their title if
strict proof is required at every step, which it may be [1]
in the absence of special conditions.

One need not dwell on the inconvenience of such a
state of things in a great commercial country. It was
amended in some particulars by an Act of 1874, which
made some of the most usual special conditions part of
the general law. The root of the evil, however, is untouched. Many times it has been proposed to establish
an official registry either of deeds or of titles. The whole
subject was elaborately considered by the Real Property
Commissioners in 1830 ; they collected much informa-

sufficiently show the vendor to have power to dispose of what he
offers to sell.

[1] The practice of conveyancers is to be content in sundry matters
with less than would be accepted as sufficient evidence in a court
of justice ; but even so the burden on the vendor under an "open
contract " is a grievous one.

tion both at home and from abroad, and recommended the establishment of a general registry ; but nothing was then done. Since that time the experiment of permissive registration of titles has twice been made, with next to no result. In 1862, in Lord Westbury's chancellorship, an office of land registry was established, and the offer of a State guaranty and great simplicity in future dealings was held out to owners who could satisfactorily prove their title. But the requirements of the initial proof were for most owners more formidable than the inconveniences of the existing system. Those inconveniences, moreover, fall chiefly and visibly not so much on existing owners as on those who buy from them ; while every man can see the mischief of exposing his own title to a rigorous official scrutiny which may disclose an unsuspected flaw, and must invite his neighbours to raise questions of boundaries. It seemed the more prudent part to let sleeping lions alone. Solicitors, again, disliked the scheme, and gave it anything but encouragement ; as with the attempt to shorten deeds, the matter was complicated by the problem of remuneration. In 1875 Lord Westbury's plan, being supposed to have failed through over-ambition, was supplanted by a more tentative and elastic one. But the office of land registry as reconstituted by Lord Cairns's Land Transfer Act, though not now, as it was for several years, an office of sinecures, is still avoided by most landowners.[1] The inevitable weakness of every scheme of merely optional

---

[1] " Registration under this Act is optional, and its success has not been sufficient to justify any lengthened account of it in an elementary work like the present": Joshua Williams on Real Property, 17th ed., by Mr. T. Cyprian Williams, 1892, p. 566.

registration is that it is not the apparent interest of the landowner, save in exceptional cases,[1] to register. It is not found in practice that the selling price of land is sensibly diminished by its being sold under special conditions of the ordinary kind. In other words, what is called a "marketable title," that is, a title such as the Court would compel a purchaser to accept upon an "open contract," is worth no more to the owner than a "good holding title," such as the vast majority of titles are. The temptation of acquiring a statutory "marketable title" is therefore spread in vain in the sight of English freeholders.

Practically the problem is unsolved. At least three distinct schools of opinion exist among competent persons, not counting those who are satisfied with things as they are. Some are for registration of title; some (now but few) are for only keeping an official record of dealings with the land; others hold that nothing effectual can, or at any rate will be done until the substance of our land laws is greatly simplified; and perhaps these last are in the right.[2] In recent years Land Transfer Bills have been promoted by Chancellors of both parties and approved by the House of Lords. They have included what may be described as a mild and modified compulsion, and a provision, adopted from the Australian colonies, for insuring registered owners against fraud or mistake by means of a special fund. This last provision is thought to be of very great utility and importance by those who have studied the "Torrens system" in detail.

---

[1] As where contiguous lands acquired under different titles are to be thrown together, and sold or let in small parcels.

[2] For references to recent literature on the subject see Note II.

Local registries of dealings with the land, not of title, were established in the last century in Middlesex and Yorkshire, and are still in use. Unfortunate decisions of the Court of Chancery made these county registers far less efficient than they were intended to be, and the Middlesex Registry is for this and other reasons worse than useless.[1] The Yorkshire Registries (one for each riding) have worked better; they have been remodelled by Acts of 1884 and 1885. Registration of assurances is well known in other English-speaking countries; it has long been in force in Ireland, in Scotland (where the system acts to a great extent as a registry of title also), and in several of the United States. Registration of title exists in most Continental countries, if not in all, and in our own Australian colonies. In England itself every manor has a register of the title to the copyhold property held of it, namely, the court rolls. But the law and the circumstances of English real property are so peculiar that the state of other lands in this respect is rather an object of envy than a presently practicable example for imitation. Neither can the archaic practice of copyhold tenure help us much. One thing seems tolerably clear: English landowners cannot both eat their cake in the form of secret conveyances, informal modes of raising money, and complicated settlements, and have their cake in the form of cheap and easy transfer of land. Either way has its advantages and its drawbacks, but we cannot follow both at once. The country must choose between them. Sir Henry Maine has pointed out that the establishment of a complete registry would tend to have con-

[1] See *Land Transfer*, 1886, p. 21.

siderable ulterior effects on legal doctrines and concep-
tions. The passage [1] should be read and considered by
every one interested in the subject. Meanwhile, we
remain in the condition very fairly described in one of
the answers sent in to the Real Property Commissioners:
"It is possible to attain to such a degree of certainty
as commonly satisfies a prudent man in the ordinary
business of life, but with considerable delay, difficulty,
and expense; the great evil is not that titles are uncertain or unsafe, but that the investigation of them is
difficult, tedious, and costly." Not many titles are
really bad, but under the existing law there must
always be an unknown element of risk.

The acquisition and proof of title to land itself, and
to rights over the land of others, have been put on a
more rational footing by the Prescription Act of 1832,
and the Real Property Limitation Acts of 1833 and
1874. Broadly stated, the results are as follows:
Twelve years' possession of land (whether it begins
with an appearance of right, or by mere intrusion or
"squatting") gives a good title as against claimants not
disabled by infancy or the like from asserting their
rights for themselves; and for the benefit of such persons or others claiming in their right, a further time of
six years is allowed, counted from the removal of the
disability or the death of the person subject to it; but
in no case may the period open for the claims of persons
out of possession be extended beyond thirty years in all
from the time when possession begins to count against
a freeholder entitled to an estate of inheritance. But
where there is a tenant for life in possession his acts or

---

[1] *Early Law and Custom*, pp. 351-61.

neglects cannot affect the title of those in remainder, and therefore when land is in settlement a much longer period may elapse before a title resting merely on adverse possession can become safe. Rights over the land of others are established by twenty years' uninterrupted enjoyment if they are easements (that is, such rights as that of passage or of having free access of light and air, which do not involve taking anything from the land), thirty years if they are profits, that is, rights of taking something off the land, of which the most familiar case is a right of common. Possession is, of course, not available as a ground of title against a person whose superior title is acknowledged, by the payment of rent for instance, by the person in actual possession. This branch of the law, even with the modern improvements, is not an elementary one; and it will be understood that there are many special points and distinctions of which I do not profess to say anything here.

It is an arguable question whether the establishment of titles by long possession is consistent with a complete and efficient system of registration. In Scotland, where there is such a system, there is nothing answering to our Statute of Limitation as regards land. And in England the Land Transfer Act of 1875 has actually excluded the operation of the Statutes of Limitation as regards land which has been put on the register. No amount of adverse possession will prevail against a registered title. This provision, which I believe is not generally known even to lawyers, makes, in the opinion of one of our most learned and experienced real property lawyers, "a vast and very mischievous change in

the law." [1]   At present "in English law, all title to land
is founded on possession," [2] and has been so for at least
seven centuries. The reversal of this principle in the
case of registered land is likely to give rise to many
difficulties apart from the danger of actual fraud. It
stereotypes all unsettled questions of boundaries, whereas
under the existing and well-understood practice they
are constantly disposed of by friendly adjustment, often
without even a formulated agreement, and in a generation or so lapse of time cures all. Those who think
that registration of title is not compatible with expecting
purchasers to satisfy themselves that the land is held in
accordance with the written title, as a prudent purchaser
always does now, seem to forget that title is not the
same thing as ownership. They have attempted to
create a system of registered ownership before the legal
profession or the public is ripe even for registered title.
More will be heard on this point before the operation of
the Land Registry is made general or compulsory.

We come now to alterations more nearly touching
the substance of the law. In 1833 the law of intestate
succession was amended in various details. It does not
seem worth while to give a particular account of either
the old or the new law. The death of a fee-simple
holder of land without making a will is in modern times
an exceptional case. Popular knowledge of the law of
descent is confined to the fundamental rule that the
eldest son (or his descendants as representing him) takes
the whole of the land to the exclusion of younger

---

[1] Sir Howard Elphinstone in *Law Quart. Rev.*, xi. 360 (Oct.
1895).

[2] Williams on Real Property, 17th ed., p. 531.

children ;[1] while daughters, on the contrary, share
equally in the absence of sons.   Nor is it often
necessary for the practising lawyer to remember the
further rules of collateral succession.   The prevalence of
settlements, and the complete freedom of disposition by
will that has existed since the Restoration, have caused
this whole head of the law to shrink into comparative
insignificance.   Nevertheless, proposals have from time
to time been made to change our unique law of inheritance as regards land by assimilating it to the law of
succession of personal property, which is substantially
the same as the Roman law in its final form and the
present law of the rest of Europe.   Throughout the
States and colonies which took their law from England
this change has already been generally made.   At home
these proposals have been strenuously resisted, and
hitherto they have always failed.   Why has a point of
comparatively slight intrinsic importance been thus made
a centre of active controversy ?   Simply because the
point actually at issue has been understood on both
sides to be the symbol of much more.   The attack was
in form directed upon a rather small anomaly ; but in
substance it was aimed at the privileges of landowners
and the custom of settling lands from generation to generation on the eldest son.   If the legal rule of primogeniture
in the strict sense were abolished, the artificial primogeniture of our family settlements could not long survive

[1] His title may be subject to the right of his father's widow to
dower, i.e. to the enjoyment of one-third of the land for her life.
But this right has become in various ways, which it would be too
long to specify, practically obsolete in England.   In the United
States it is still active, and is the subject of quite modern text-
books.

it. Immovable property would become assimilated to movable both in law and in sentiment; or to speak more correctly, the change in the law would be an all but conclusive mark that public feeling was changed already. As it is, by far the greater number of the well-to-do people who make wills (I say well-to-do, because so much may fairly be inferred from a man sending his will to be settled by a conveyancing counsel) throw their land into a common stock with the rest of their property for equal division among their children. What is called "making an eldest son" is the exception. Sometimes the proposal to abolish the rule of primogeniture on intestacy, leaving intact the power of disposal by will in favour of the eldest son or any one else, is confounded with a proposal to introduce compulsory division of the whole or some considerable part of the heritage, according to the system which has always prevailed on the Continent. An error of such magnitude barely needs, one would think, to be pointed out. The two plans belong to different orders of legal institutions. Since Tory Ministers have proposed the abolition of primogeniture (this first happened in 1887), its most ardent supporters can hardly expect to see it last much longer. Already the Intestates Estates Act, 1890, gives land as well as personal property to a widow, if there are no children, where the husband has died intestate and worth less than £500 in all.

Copyhold lands have been incidentally mentioned in their historical aspect in former chapters. Many of their incidents are relics of an antiquity to which the Norman Conquest is a thing of yesterday. But however venerable its antiquity, and however interesting to the student of historical jurisprudence the evidence which it preserves, this tenure is found in many ways inconvenient in modern practice; nor is the advantage of copyhold titles being registered on the court rolls of the manor sufficient to outweigh the inconveniences. From imperfect identification of boundaries, and for other reasons, dealings with property of which part is freehold and part copyhold (a very common case) are apt to be exceedingly troublesome. The fines and other payments due from the tenant to the lord of the manor are mostly not a serious burden, but they may be so in exceptional cases. On the whole, the conversion of copyhold into freehold tenure, for which the proper word is enfranchisement, is generally felt to be desirable. It could always be done by agreement between the lord and the tenant; but the lord had to be willing, and the tenant as well as the lord under no disability, to say nothing of the possibility of disagreement as to the terms on which the lord's rights were to be extinguished. Under certain modern Acts of Parliament, of which the principal one was passed in 1852, enfranchisement is now compulsory on the requisition of either the lord or the tenant. Provision is made for valuing the manorial rights if the parties cannot agree. By the operation of these Acts copyhold tenure is gradually but surely disappearing; and its end is being hastened by yet further legislation.

A series of Acts, now consolidated by the Copyhold Act, 1894,[1] have increased the facilities for enfranchisement in various ways. Every new copyholder must have express notice that he is entitled to

[1] 57 & 58 Vict. c. 46. The latest and most important of the consolidated Acts was passed in 1887.

enfranchise his land on paying the lord's compensation
and the steward's fees; those fees are defined by a new
scale; additional provisions are made for the assessment
of compensation to the lord, and paying it in the form
of a rent-charge [1] with an option to the tenant to redeem
at twenty-five years' purchase; and in certain cases the
Board of Agriculture (formerly the Land Commissioners)
has power to enfranchise the copyholds of a manor
bodily if such is the desire of two-thirds of the copyholders.   Any rights of common which may be attached
to copyhold tenures are expressly saved from being
prejudiced by the change of tenure.

If one form of ancient customary law is becoming
obsolete in copyholds, there is another branch of the
same stock which, within the memory of the present
generation, has been called into fresh life, and recovered
much of its old importance: I speak of the law concerning rights of common.   Such rights may be
regarded as the remnant of the ancient communal
system of holding and cultivating land.   Being useless
to modern agriculture, and inconvenient for the larger
landowners, they were long looked upon with disfavour
by both the judges and the legislature, and were in
a way to disappear even faster than copyhold tenure,
but for the discovery that they were a valuable means
of securing open spaces for public exercise and recreation.   Two or three centuries ago, it is almost needless
to say, there was no lack of open spaces even in London,
nor any visible prospect of it.   Wholesale inclosure,

[1] Such rent-charges, though doubtless discoverable by application to the Board, may in course of time be lions in the path to
subsequent purchasers, not knowing (as they sometimes well may
not) that the land was ever copyhold.

begun in more or less irregular ways in the sixteenth
century, was the deliberate policy of the social reformers
and philanthropists of the eighteenth. To bring as
much land as possible under cultivation seemed to them
the just ambition of the landowner who would serve
the commonwealth. As long ago as the thirteenth
century the statute of Merton had authorised the lords
of manors to "approve,"[1] that is, inclose for their own
profit, as much of the waste land as would leave enough
uninclosed for the use of the commoners.[2] Inclosures
might also be made without limit if the consent of all
persons entitled to rights of common was obtained;
but this was seldom practicable. Many commons were
inclosed under local Acts of Parliament, and by various
old statutes inclosure for particular purposes, such as
planting timber, was encouraged. In 1801 a general
Inclosure Act was passed (superseded by a completer

---

[1] "Approve" in this sense is not the common word = Lat.
approbare, neither does it stand for appropriare, as has been con-
jectured with some plausibility. It represents an old French verb,
aprouer or approuer, to profit or enrich, from preu or prou, itself an
obscure word, which in modern French survives in "ni prou ni
peu" (cf. preux, prouesse). In Latin of the late thirteenth century
(Statute of Westminster and Fleta) it appears in reflexive construction as se appruare. "Se appruare de" . . . is therefore "to
make one's profit of" . . . exactly what in the Statute of Merton,
where the word itself does not occur, is expressed by the phrase
"commodum suum facere." The corresponding substantive is
"approment" or "approwement" in the English of the fifteenth
and sixteenth centuries. In the seventeenth century the spelling
approve, approvement, and with it the mistaken derivation from approbare, came in. See the words in the Oxford English Dictionary.

[2] It has been doubted whether the law declared by the statute
was really new: Joshua Williams on "Rights of Common," pp. 107,
108; Elton on "Commons and Waste Lands," 177-86; but see
Pollock and Maitland, Hist. Eng. Law, i. 612.

measure in 1845), and a standing commission was established to conduct and regulate the inclosure of common lands. The object of this policy was not merely to bring fresh land into cultivation, but also, and as regards the Act of 1845 chiefly,[1] to get rid of the old customs of cultivation by scattered parcels or shifting allotments in common fields. In 1845, however, there was already a kind of presentiment of coming change; for village greens were specially saved, and the inclosure of land near large towns was made subject to the consent of Parliament—a consent which some years later was made necessary in all cases. Provision was also made for the devotion of part of the land to public purposes. The Act, however, was still entitled "An Act to facilitate the inclosure and improvement of commons and lands held in common."

The reversal of the inclosing policy may be dated from 1865. Towards that time the rapid increase of building in the neighbourhood of London conferred a new value on lands which had been worthless to the lords, and created a new danger to the people, who saw themselves being deprived of their playgrounds. The cause of the commoners became the cause of the public. Litigation ensued about various common lands, Hampstead Heath among others. In 1865 a Committee of the House of Commons considered the question of preserving open spaces near London, and the Commons Preservation Society was founded by private exertions. In the following year the Metropolitan Commons Act,

---

[1] This appears from the proceedings of the Select Committee in 1884. Probably most of the earlier special Inclosure Acts had the same character. Cp. Seebohm, *English Village Community*, p. 14.

1866, put a stop to further inclosures within the
metropolitan police district, and empowered the Inclosure Commissioners [1] to prepare schemes for the
management and regulation of the commons thus
preserved. Some commons, Wimbledon, for example,
were separately dealt with by special Acts.

Meanwhile the movement for reviving and maintain-
ing rights of common was extended into the country
parts. At Berkhamstead an attempted encroachment
on the lord's part was vigorously and successfully
resisted. Mr. Augustus Smith, a tenant of the manor,
who fortunately had the means of doing right to himself
and his fellows, sent down men by train early in the
morning, who in a couple of hours demolished about a
mile of wire fence erected by the then Earl Brownlow,
taking care (as persons abating an unlawful obstruction
or inclosure always should) to do no unnecessary damage
to the materials. In the litigation that ensued Mr.
Smith satisfied the Court of Chancery that his action
was lawful, and obtained a decree against any repetition
of the encroachment. A series of contests followed, in
which the commoners were for the most part, though
not uniformly, victorious. In 1871 the rule was
declared and acted on by Lord Hatherley, then Chancellor, that, where rights of common were shown to
have been claimed and exercised for many years, it was
the duty of the Court to find, if possible, an account of
their origin which would justify them in law. Not
that Lord Hatherley professed to lay down any new
principle, but there can be no doubt that in fact he

[1] This body has been transformed first into the Land Commissioners and then into the Board of Agriculture.

dealt with the case in a very different spirit from that
of the judges of the Elizabethan age.[1] In 1874 the
case of Epping Forest was taken up by the City of
London. Here the peculiar and once oppressive rights
of the Crown under the old forest law were made to
play an unexpected part in restraining encroachments
on the common. Owners and occupiers of land within
a royal forest were subject by that law to various
burdens and restrictions ; thus they might not have
fences above a height fitted to allow free passage to
deer ; and by way of compensation they were allowed
rights of common, subject to the forest rules, over the
whole waste of the forest without regard to the
boundaries of particular manors. This was an insuper-
able bar to the lord of a small or decayed manor lawfully making himself absolute owner of the waste, as
has not unfrequently been done elsewhere, by buying
up the remaining rights of common. By a mere accident
the Corporation of London were owners of a small
property within the bounds of the Forest, and were
thus entitled to undertake, as no private commoner
could effectually have done, the research and expense
necessary to establish their rights to the full extent.
At the instance of the lords themselves, who thought

[1] Warrick v. Queen's College, Oxford, L. R. 6 Ch. 716. In the
later case of Goodman v. Mayor of Saltash, 7 App. Ca. 633 (1882),
a still further application of this principle was made by the House
of Lords. The decision established a right (nominally for inhabitants of Saltash, practically for the public) to take oysters in the
Tamar. I am disposed to think the reasoning by which it was
arrived at may be found to support claims to rights over land also,
which have hitherto been supposed incapable of legal existence ;
this, however, is too speculative a question to dwell upon here,
nor have any recent decisions thrown light upon it.

they were choosing the lesser risk, measures were taken
by Parliament for preserving the waste land not yet
inclosed; but the lawsuit of 1874 (the course of which
Parliament refused to stop) showed that many of the
inclosures made within the previous twenty years, and
untouched by the Act of Parliament, were unlawful.
In the result a considerable amount of space (estimated
at more than 2000 acres) was not only preserved but
restored to the public.[1] Meanwhile the Parliamentary
Commission proceeded with its work, and in 1878 a
new Act of Parliament constituted the Corporation of
London conservators of the Forest, with full powers of
regulation and management, and with the charge of
preserving it "uninclosed and unbuilt on, as an open
space for the recreation and enjoyment of the public."[2]

In 1876 a general Commons Act was passed, which
took the great step of establishing a presumption for
rural as well as suburban commons in favour of regulation rather than inclosure. Improvement is expressly
defined so to include adding to the beauty of a common,
a thing never dreamt of in the former Inclosure Acts.
Special provision is made for giving facilities for recreation and preserving objects of historical interest. In
short, the Act, even where it leaves most to administrative discretion, is an emphatic instruction to the Inclosure

[1] See for further details the Report of the Commons Preservation Society, 1877, which is to be had for 6d.
[2] 41 & 42 Vict. c. cexiii. Outstanding questions were by the
same Act referred to the absolute arbitration of Sir A. (now Lord)
Hobhouse. "All questions of importance in relation to the Forest
are now settled, and the arbitrator has made his final award, specifying by a map the lands confided to the care of the Corporation
of London, and dedicated to the public enjoyment for ever."—
(Report of Commons Preservation Society, 1882.)

Commissioners to reverse the policy of the earlier part of the century. Among other points which mark a new spirit, it makes encroachment on village greens a public nuisance. The general interest in these matters has continued to increase. Local associations for the preservation of commons and footpaths have been formed in several parts of the country. In some cases they have effectually withstood encroachment; in others the mere knowledge of their existence has probably prevented it; sometimes they have been able to promote the adjustment of disputed rights in the interest of the public and all parties.

Finally the Statute of Merton, though not repealed, has been rendered practically inoperative, "approvement" being no longer valid without the consent of the Board of Agriculture.[1]

A new form of encroachment has lately been found to require new vigilance. Railway companies and such like bodies are prone to put forth their hands on common rather than on inclosed land when there appears to be any choice, that they may have the less compensation to pay; and their managers naturally take little thought for preserving the beauty or the quietness of the country affected by their schemes. But several projects of this kind have been signally discomfited in Parliament; and when, at the twenty-first meeting of the Commons Preservation Society in 1886, the work done by it since its foundation was summed up by Mr. Shaw-Lefevre and Mr. Bryce, Mr. Bryce was able to say "the railways have begun to fear us."[2]

---

[1] Law of Commons Amendment Act, 1893. The whole history may be seen more at large in Mr. Shaw-Lefevre's *English Commons and Forests.* [2] Report of Proceedings, 1885-86, p. 34.

Important as the reaction against inclosure of open land may justly be thought, it has, on the whole, been effected through change in the spirit and working of the law rather than by changes in the law itself. One remarkable case of recent change remains to be noticed, —a case where, after the law had repeatedly been declared by persons speaking with authority to be perfect and in no need of reform, a large measure of reform, designed by the greatest lawyer of the Conservative party, was accepted almost without a whisper of opposition. We have seen what grievous dislike was incurred by strict settlements of land when they were a novelty. Coke and Bacon, opponents in most things, agreed in denouncing them. Pamphleteers wished "that there might be no estate but absolute, for life or inheritance, without conditions or entails . . . and this would shorten all suits about estates."[1] Until the close of the seventeenth century the judges followed the Chancellor's allowance of the new-fashioned dispositions with undisguised reluctance. But when once the rule against perpetuities was fixed, the landowners and conveyancers had things all their own way for some generations. The scheme of settlement devised by certain ingenious counsellors of the Restoration passed, in the esteem of landowners and even of lawyers, into the category of things immemorial and sacred, bulwarks of Church and State. The Real Property Commissioners could find no fault in it. Lord St. Leonards, a score of years later, was of the same mind. Objections could, in his view, proceed only from ignorance or perversity. In such words as these he expounded to the English landowner (the

[1] 3 *Jurid. Soc. Papers*, 598.

farmer had then hardly entered into his reckoning) the
beatitudes of an English settled estate :—

"A desire has often been shown, not merely to improve the law of real property, but unnecessarily to alter
it, and to admit only simple settlements after the fashion
of the Code Napoléon.   But the present plan of a strict
settlement in this country is free from all objection.   It
does not place land *extra commercium*, but within reasonable limits enables the owner to transmit it to all his
posterity ; and from its very nature leads to successive
settlements, which alone have kept many estates in the
same families. . . .

"Thus are estates quickly resettled, and the State
does not, that I am aware of, suffer any inconvenience
from such repeated settlements.   No man in this country
can justly complain that there is not sufficient land in
the market on sale. . . .

"It is objected that these purposes are effected by a
complicated and an expensive machinery ; but who ever
complained of the complex movements in a well-finished
watch ?   We admire the connection of its parts depending on each other, and all necessary to form the combination which produces the desired results."

Metaphors are dangerous things.   A well-finished
watch is desirable not for the beauty of its machinery,
but that its wearer may know the time of day.   He will
prefer a cheap watch that keeps fair time to a sidereal
chronometer which is out of relation to men's common
count of hours.   Moreover, a watch is far from being a
perfect machine ; the watchmaking trade is peculiar in
its constitution and division of labour, and improvements
have been introduced only slowly and with great diffi-

culty. But this elaborate combination, it is said, "produces the desired results." Desired by whom and for whom? There is the point.

Behind the question of legal machinery there is the question of social policy, which has gradually been forcing itself on men's attention, Lord St. Leonards and other persons of authority notwithstanding. The results of a strict settlement are doubtless desired by its makers, and the purpose is effected with exceeding skill. But are they desirable for the common weal? Dealing with the land is hampered; not made impossible or impracticable, as sometimes appears to be thought, at least not if the settlement is framed by competent hands; but hampered it is, and it is idle to deny it. Powers of sale and management are useful, but they are not ownership. I have power to consult any book in a great law library by walking a few score paces from my chambers. But if there is a book I should rather like to consult, but can do without, the chances are that I shall not go. Every scholar knows the difference between having books at one's elbow and having to go out to see them. So it is with attempts to restore the uses of absolute ownership after dismembering its substance.

And there is a still graver economical objection to strict settlements than any real or supposed want of power to deal with the land. It is that they destroy the ordinary means and motives of an owner for dealing with it in the way of improvement. The life-tenant of a settled estate, "limited owner," as he is expressively called in modern Acts of Parliament, seldom has any capital to put into the land. Incumbrances created by previous settlements commonly leave no margin of revenue beyond what is needed for barely keeping up the estate. And if the limited owner has other means, he is still without much inducement to apply them to the improvement of the estate ; if he does so, he spends for the exclusive benefit of an eldest son who is already preferred by the settlement. He is much more likely to use his money for the benefit of younger children ; and justly, so far as they and he are concerned ; but this divorce of capital from land is a loss to the land itself, to the cultivator, and in the long run to the commonwealth.

Much has been said and written of the evils of strict settlement since the renewal of law reform which began about sixty years ago, and sundry partial measures have been taken to palliate them. It is needless to describe these, for they have been mostly superseded by the Settled Land Act of 1882, due to Lord Cairns as its chief author, the object of which is to confer on "limited owners" as large and effectual powers of using the land to the best advantage as are compatible with settlements existing at all. By this Act a tenant for life [1] has powers of selling and leasing, and other powers of administration, without any special provision in the settlement, and, subject to certain safeguards intended to prevent abuse, and not burdensome, he may exercise them at his own discretion. He cannot, however, sell a principal mansion-house or heirlooms without leave of the Court. His powers cannot be released or bargained away, and no disposition purporting to abrogate or

---

[1] Certain other limited owners, whose position differs only technically from that of a tenant for life, are included in the Act. There are later amending Acts of too detailed and technical a nature to call for notice here.

restrain them is valid. The purchase-money of land
sold under the Act may be spent (among other purposes)
on the discharge of incumbrances, or on improvements of several specified kinds. Expenditure on improvements is subject to the control of either the Land
Commissioners (a body constituted by the amalgamation
of the former Inclosure, Copyhold, and Tithe Com-
missions) or the Court. No power is given to raise
money from the land by mortgage as distinct from sale
in order to execute improvements on it; this can be
done, by a somewhat tedious process, under an Act of
1864. The list of authorised improvements, however,
is extended by the Settled Land Act. It must be observed that the Act does not alter the beneficial title to
the settled land, or the investments representing its
value, or the increased value given to part of the land
with money obtained by selling another part. The
tenant for life cannot enlarge his own interest; he can
only decide in what form the property shall be handed
on to those who come after him. He may leave them
fewer acres with equal or greater value, in the shape
either of incumbrances taken off or of improvements
added. He may even leave them money instead of
land. So far he can alter the subject-matter of their
rights, but the rights themselves he cannot touch. It
was reserved for another Tory Lord Chancellor in 1887
to carry through the House of Lords a proposal for
the automatic expansion of estates tail into fee simple.
Even this, however, would in the main operate as a
simplification of form. The authors of the Land Transfer Bill professed not to interfere with the general
principle of family settlements.

It is still too early to say what will be the economical effects of the Settled Land Act. No such carefully devised measure of administrative reform in our land laws has been passed since the Fines and Recoveries Act. Probably its framers have succeeded in their intention of removing every obstacle to dealing with settled land that is not involved in the very existence of settlements. Experience must show how far the country will be satisfied. Reforms of this kind are most useful for their time, and their promoters deserve all honour. But they all add to the complications of a system already too complex; and the day seems to be at hand when the system will no longer bear this process, and reconstruction must be faced.

The traditions of English character, the circumstances of an age of commerce, and the example of other English-speaking communities, all seem to point to the simplification of landholding and the encouragement of absolute ownership. On the other hand, there are certain speculative reformers, of late very loud and busy, who will have it that private ownership of land is altogether wrong, and instead of desiring that, so far as may be, every man should be his own landlord, are for making the State every man's landlord. To discuss such schemes is not within my province. As Lord Hobhouse has well said,[1] "they are hardly proposals for the alteration of the laws relating to land, or of any other branch of municipal law commonly so called; but rather for shifting the very basis of English society, and remodelling it on different theories of property, and of the relation between the State and individuals."

---

[1] *The Dead Hand*, 1880, p. 164.

It will be time for lawyers to take a serious view of what is barbarously called "Land Nationalisation" (but it deserves a barbarous name) when its advocates have shown themselves capable, as thus far they have not, of appreciating the enormous difficulties that would beset an attempt to give tangible form to their vast and vague idea. No law could be framed for destroying private property in land, or (what some of these reformers take to be the root of mischief) the relation of landlord and tenant, without hundreds of keen-witted men forthwith setting themselves to evade it. The history we have surveyed has given us, perhaps, examples enough of what happens when the letter of laws is matched against the nature of man and of things.

As to the question of public economy, I have nothing to say of it. Not only is it not my business here, but I cannot imagine that those who were not convinced by Mr. Fawcett[1] are likely to be convinced by anything I could add. It is said that working men in London are found apt to be taken with these projects of national socialism. It may be so; too few of them are ballasted in their course by much, or any, of the magic of owner-ship. But the artisans of the north country are already in great part, through the operation of building societies, full owners of the homes they dwell in. Let such a working man understand that our new social reformers will confiscate his well-earned cottage neither more nor less than the squire's mansion and the manufacturer's mill—that he too is to become a rent-paying tenant of the State, or a so-called occupying owner taxed up to

[1] "State Socialism and the Nationalisation of Land," Macmillan's Magazine, July 1883 (since republished in pamphlet form).

tho rental value of his holding—and I think he will prefer his risks of poverty to such progress as the social enthusiasts of the East or the West have to offer him. The extreme Socialists, after threatening in brave words to extinguish both the great historical parties of our Commonwealth, have now (1895) been signally rebuffed by the electors of Great Britain,[1] and have lost what little representation in Parliament they had snatched in the last few years. We may be permitted to trust that the progress of English laws and society will be, as it has been, in a steady course of rational reform; that men of power and wisdom may be with us in time of need in the future as they have been in the past; and that the terrible fascination of revolution may remain, as it yet is, alien and impotent among our people.

> Dea magna dea Cybebe, dea domina Dindymi,
> procul a mea tuus sit furor omnis, era, domo :
> alios age incitatos, alios age rabidos.

---

[1] In Ireland there has never yet been room for them.

APPENDIX

NOTE A.—THE GERMANIC LAND SYSTEM

Few passages have been more discussed than the short account of early German agriculture in the *Germania* of Tacitus (c. 26). The best exposition is still, perhaps, that of Waitz (*Deutsche Verfassungs-Geschichte*, vol. i., p. 104 sqq., ed. 1865). There are some useful notes in Mr. H. Furneaux' recent edition of the book (Oxford, 1894). The critical words are these :—

" Agri pro numero cultorum ab universis vicis [al. in vices] occupantur, quos mox inter se secundum dignationem partiuntur. Facilitatem partiendi camporum spatia praestant. Arva per annos mutant, et superest ager."

I would translate to this effect : " The German township as a whole takes up a tract of land according to the number of its husbandmen. The land so occupied is then allotted among the members in proportion to their rank, the extent of open ground making this process a simple one. The parcels under the plough are shifted yearly, and there is land to spare."

First, what does *universi* mean ? It might mean a whole tribe or nation, a State, as we may fairly call it, if we remember that it was not organised like the modern State. But the partition of lands, newly occupied or otherwise, between individual cultivators is the work not of the State, but of the smaller community which appears on various scales and under various names, and for English purposes may best be called a township. It is possible, and indeed

probable, that from the earliest times not only the kings but
other great men had large portions of the land allotted to
them in separate lordship. Such men were not members,
but lords of the communities which might be settled on
their lands. But it is also probable from what follows that
it is a communal system that Tacitus here has in view.

The alternative reading has much more MS. authority for
it, *vicis* being the reading of only one MS. But, though it
is defended with great ingenuity by Orelli (1848), and is
tempting in some ways, it makes a difficult and ambiguous
sentence. It would imply that (1) Tacitus was at a loss to
give a more definite name than *universi* to the German
agricultural unit ; (2) the same ground was successively taken
up by different communities. We should thus get, at first
sight, a closer agreement with Cæsar's account (B. G. vi. 22,
quoted in Stubbs's Sel. Ch. p. 53). But it is by no means clear
that Tacitus meant to agree with Cæsar, who appears rather
to be describing clans still in a nomadic stage, while Tacitus
seems to be speaking of the permanent settlement of fresh
tracts, "new takes," as they say on Dartmoor.

As to the process of partition, it is clear that already
there were distinct degrees of rank, that the more worshipful
man got more land allotted to him, and the less worshipful
less. "Arva per annos mutant" is taken by the best modern
authorities to refer to the course of husbandry, and signify
the alternation of crop and fallow. But it may also import
(what seems otherwise probable) that every man had, or might
have, a different parcel allotted to him each year. In like
manner "superest ager" may refer to the unallotted common
land of the township, or to vacant land not yet appropriated
by any township, or to both.

Fustel de Coulanges considered this passage of Tacitus in
his *Recherches sur quelques problèmes d'histoire*, Paris, 1885. He
thinks that Tacitus wrote it for the information of Roman
readers as farmers rather than as publicists, and that this
accounts for the want of technical definition which has given
so much trouble to modern commentators. "Tous les termes
se rapportent à la culture." It is quite true that the leading
word *occupantur* expresses a bare fact, and does not involve

any particular inference as to the kind of right in which the acts are done ; on the other hand it does not exclude any which is otherwise plausible. References to recent criticism of Fustel's work may be found in the Introduction to the French translation of Maine's *Village Communities*, sub tit. *Études sur l'histoire du droit*, Paris, 1889. An article in the *Quarterly Review* for October 1896 opens an interesting field of comparison, and a new one to most English readers at any rate, on the history of land communities in Spain.

Note B.—Symbolic Transfer in Early English Customs

Professor Sohm, following K. Maurer and Schmid, assumes that the A.S. "book" was the common mode of assurance, and goes so far as to deny that symbolical transfers were used at all before the Conquest. (*Fränkisches Recht und römisches Recht*, Weimar, 1880, p. 30.) But the absence of records appears quite inconclusive. It was not a native Anglo-Saxon or Germanic custom, but a foreign practice introduced under clerical influence "iuxta exempla Romanorum," to keep any written records at all. Besides, it is not the case that we find before the Conquest "keine Spur der Investitur." There are half a dozen examples in the *Cod. Dipl.* See Nos. 18, *37, 104, 114, *177, 1019. In No. 114 a sod from the place is expressed to be delivered along with the book. In the other cases it is mentioned to have been placed on the altar or on the book of the Gospels. Two of the charters, here also noted by an asterisk, are marked by Kemble as forgeries. But the like incident must have been found in genuine originals which the forger was imitating. Two other cases may be added from the Black Book of Peterborough, in a record printed by Dr. Stubbs in 1861, and accepted by him as genuine. Early in the eighth century "Æthelred, the glorious king of Mercia, on the occasion of a visit to Medeshamstede, gave to the brethren he found there thirty mancuses at Lengtricdun, and confirmed the gift by placing on the Gospels' Book a sod taken from the place." Again, a purchase of lands at Cedonasde from the king "was ratified at Tonitun (Northampton ?) in the king's chamber by joining of hands, and by placing a sod from Cedenanác on the Gospels' Book, in the presence of Bishop Saxulf." Here we seem to catch the very moment of the final struggle of the older symbolical ceremony with the "book," which for great occasions was to supersede it—if, indeed, it did so; for, as Palgrave has observed (*Proofs and Illustrations*, ccxxviii.), the silence of most charters as to any symbolical delivery really proves nothing. My own belief is that for the common occasions of private persons the symbolical transfer never went out of use. It seems to me no extravagant supposition that many of the symbolical customs still found in copyholds, such as surrender by a straw in the manor of Winteringham, in Lincolnshire (*Academy*, Nov. 19, 1881, p. 386), are really of immemorial antiquity. On Sohm's and Schmid's theory they would be late medieval imitations of the Franco-Norman custom.

It seems far-fetched, however, to find in the laws of Alfred an attempt to convert book-land into family or customary land by way of reaction towards pure Teutonic principles (Mr. Lodge in *Essays in Anglo-Saxon Law*, pp. 70, 71). The law says that a man who has inherited book-land from his kindred must not give it from the family "if there be writing or *witness* that it was forbidden by those men who at first acquired it, and by those who gave it to him, that he should do so." Probably this was only a confirmation of existing law (compare the preamble), and it rather goes to show that restrictive clauses were often disregarded than anything else. But it does seem to allow validity to restrictions of this kind not expressed in the book itself, but only declared by the donor in the presence of witnesses—a point not noticed by Mr. Lodge. So far we may say that the peculiar quality and privileges of book-land were kept in check by the old family principles.

NOTE C.—THE ORIGINS OF THE MANOR

It may be useful to state in a summary way the different

theories as to the origin of manorial tenures and customs which have prevailed among English authors at different times. For shortness' sake they will have to be put rather in their extreme forms than with the reserves and qualifications which their more cautious maintainers have introduced. But this will not involve any injustice, for the object is not to give an exact account of this or that author's opinions, but to indicate the successive tendencies of historical speculation, the changes of fashion, as one might say, if the dignity of history suffered it. Those who desire a more careful and detailed study of the different schools may find it in the Introduction to Mr. Paul Vinogradoff's *Villainage in England*, and Dr. Andrews' work on *The Old English Manor*.[1]

Down to the middle of this century, or later, the common opinion, founded probably on Blackstone's account, was that at the date of the Norman Conquest, and for some centuries afterwards, the greater part of English land was held at the absolute will and pleasure of the lords of manors. The medieval customs evidenced in surveys and court rolls were supposed to have arisen (so far as any rights of the tenant were concerned) out of mere sufferance, "by a long series of immemorial encroachments on the lord."[2] It was not uncommonly stated or assumed that before the Conquest the land was to a great extent in the hands of free yeomen or peasant proprietors. These were supposed to have been either evicted or reduced to villenage by the Norman lords, leaving little or no trace in records of the Anglo-Norman or any later period.

Kemble's great work, *The Saxons in England*, was published in 1848, but the opinions of his school were not fully established in the acceptance of scholars and the general use of teachers till about twenty years later. However, the acceptance, when it fairly set in, was so complete and un-

[1] Mr. Scrutton's *Commons and Common Fields* (Cambridge, 1887) may also be usefully consulted.
[2] Blackstone's *Comm.*, i. 95. It is not clear whether Blackstone thought this process dated from before the Conquest or not, but I think he would not have put it much before in any case.

questioning as almost to invite a reaction. According to
this school the original type of the Germanic community
was, among the Saxon conquerors of Britain as elsewhere,
an association of free men equal in rights, if not in social
rank or wealth. The village or township was a group of
joint owners, acknowledging no superior except for military
service and other purposes of public order and justice, and
regulating its own internal affairs. Personal lordship, however, was among the early Germanic institutions, and
territorial lordship was already growing up some considerable time before the Conquest ;[1] in fact feudalism was
impending, and the Conquest only accelerated the reception
and definition of feudal rules. Probably no serious writer
of this school would have denied that many details remained
obscure as to dates and otherwise. Nevertheless it was
agreed in the main that, whether the process began earlier
or later, servile tenants did not encroach on the lords as
supposed by Blackstone and the modern law-books, but on
the contrary the lords encroached on rights and liberties of
the occupiers, which were more ancient than their own. It
was not disputed that the Saxon freemen, like the citizens
of a Greek or Roman city, had below them a considerable
class of unfree men, slaves in fact. This indeed has never
been disputed by any one, though in some popular descriptions of the free village community the existence of slavery
may have been allowed to fall a good deal into the background. The German word "mark" and the phrase "mark
system" were freely adopted by writers of this school, and
their doctrine is often called the "mark theory," though
there is really no English authority for the use of "mark"
as a synonym of "village community" or "township."
Maine's *Village Communities* is justly esteemed the best
general exposition of the theory for English readers, and
this for the very reason that Sir Henry Maine professed,

---

[1] In Kemble's view (*Saxons in England*, i. 307), "the ruin of
the free cultivators and the overgrowth of the lords" had already
gone far before the time of Æthelred. In other words, the ancient
free institutions had broken down at least a century before the
Normans came. (Cp. Freeman, *N. C.* v. 462.)

as regards European institutions, only to take the results of the prevailing Germanic school as he found them. It must be added that this school has never regarded the village community, township, or " mark," as a mere association of other-wise unconnected households or individuals, like a modern club or commercial company. Some bond of kinship, traditional if not absolutely historical, is always understood to have made the association possible in the first instance. Kemble and Maine are both express, nay emphatic, on this point.[1] It is needless to remind educated readers how in-timately it is connected with the importance of Adoption in archaic societies. A fictitious brotherhood was the founda-tion of the Germanic comitatus, and played a considerable part in the early stages of feudalism, as M. Flach has lately shown.

The Blackstonian theory (as we may call it for con-venience) had taken its facts from the legal formulas of the later Middle Ages, as interpreted by the still later classical text-writers of English law. The Germanic theory, dis-carding this unreal treatment of a large and complex historical process, corrected the former view, as we have just seen, by taking account of political and economic develop-ments, and bringing the purely English history into line with the general mass of Teutonic learning and tradition. But the later extensions of this method in such hands as Nasse's[2] prepared the way for a critical reaction.

It was found that close attention to the details of medi-eval agriculture and administration raised new problems which the Germanists, if not as unconscious of them as the Blackstonians, had left in the background. Anglo-Saxon documents, when they do go into detail, show us the tillers of the soil in a condition not materially different from the villenage of the thirteenth century. The labour-dues, well-known in post-Norman inquests and court rolls, are there; a lord to whom they are rendered is there; the highly

[1] See especially Kemble's Appendix A on patronymic place-names.
[2] *The Agricultural Community of the Middle Ages.* (Eng. trans. by Col. Ouvry, Cobden Club, 1871.)

artificial system of common-field cultivation, though not
described in terms, is plainly there too when one has learnt
to trace it.[1]   Free communities are not visibly there, only
supposed survivals of ancient freedom, which after all may
be regarded as ambiguous.   Hence, when Teutonic enthusi-
asm and the brilliance of Kemble's exposition had spent
their early charms, the question became inevitable : Was
the free village community ever there at all ?   Why should
not the usual medieval relations between the lord of a
manor and his tenants in villenage be as old as anything
else in the manorial system ?   Is not the whole system really
of one piece ?   These and such like points were raised by
Mr. Seebohm's work in this country.   Soon after his *English
Village Community* had begun to engage serious attention,
M. Fustel de Coulanges independently attacked the German
school on the Continent.   In addition to destructive criticism
of the German "mark theory," some writers, and notably
Fustel, have undertaken to maintain that the supposed
Teutonic village community is nothing but a continuation of
the Roman *villa*, which beyond any doubt was a great man's
estate cultivated by servile work.   Neither Fustel's methods
nor his results have been generally accepted in his own
country.   M. Paul Viollet, M. Flach, M. Dareste, and M.
Glasson, have all criticised his work (partly by way of self-
defence) with more or less severity, and have pointed out that,
although he constantly and justly insisted on strict accuracy
in distinguishing fact from conjecture, his own use of authorities was not always adequate or even exact.   M. Flach is of
opinion that even in Gaul there was nothing like a general
survival of Roman municipal institutions.   It is to be
observed, in any case, that Fustel de Coulanges never
examined English facts or documents himself, nor, so far as
I know, expressed any opinion whether his conclusions, which
were strictly limited to the materials before him, would be
applicable to the English settlement in Britain.   Whoever
wishes to rely on Fustel's work for English purposes ought

---

[1] This is less material ; for if there were no Anglo-Saxon
evidence at all it would be impossible to believe that such a system
was introduced after the Conquest.

to be prepared to show that the determining conditions, as to the continuity of Roman institutions and otherwise, were not materially different in Britain and in Gaul; and Mr. Ashley, now of Harvard University, the only English writer who has followed Fustel without reserve, has not to my knowledge attempted anything of the kind. Thus the new "villa" school of early English history, if one may call it so by way of contrast to the "mark" school, is a Romanising one, and stands more or less committed to alliance with the late Mr. Coote and other students who have from time to time endeavoured to show that the persistence of Roman elements in our civilisation has been underrated. Much learning and ingenuity have been spent on this endeavour. Without entering here on the subject,[1] I am bound to state it as my considered opinion that on the whole this expenditure has been in vain. It is possible, however, to deny or not to be satisfied that free village communities existed in England within historic times, and yet not to accept the proposed derivation of the dependent community from the Roman villa. Maine has suggested with much force[2] that it may have been the Roman villa that was influenced by the barbarian village, Teutonic or other. It would be quite natural for the internal economy of a great Roman estate in the provinces, or even in Italy, to be modelled to some extent on the customs with which the majority of the slaves doing out-door work had been familiar in their old homes.

The "villa" theory may be said to be, to a limited extent, a restoration of the Blackstonian or older manorial theory. So far as the facts from the Conquest to the thirteenth or fourteenth century are concerned, its upholders agree with Blackstone in regarding the law of the king's judges as a correct expression of those facts. But, instead of holding that both facts and law dated from the Norman Conquest, this theory carries them back as far as the English conquest of Britain. There seems to be in this school a tendency, and almost an avowed wish, to encourage modern optimist views of social progress by representing the tillers of the soil as

[1] Cp. Andrews, *The Old English Manor*, pp. 34-40.
[2] *Early Law and Custom*, p. 351.

moving slowly but steadily throughout the early Middle
Ages from a worse to a better position. Its adherents are
therefore really very far from having returned to the Blackstonian point of view ; they take in a much wider field, and
aim at much more complete explanation.   They have
certainly done good by demanding and enforcing a fresh
examination of the evidence.   And Mr. Seebohm has been
the first modern writer to exhibit and prove what a yardland
in the common fields really was.[1]   Meanwhile the conclusions
of this school cannot be said to have established themselves
either here or on the Continent.   Mr. Elton,[2] Mr. Kenelm
Digby,[3] and, I think, most of our legal scholars, adhere to
the Germanic doctrine in the main, though not to the in-
cautious generalities of secondhand expounders which are
still repeated now and again in semi-popular writings.   From
Russia the Germanic champions are reinforced by Mr.
Vinogradoff and Mr. Kovalevsky, — strong allies both,
Vinogradoff with a knowledge of the English documents,
published and unpublished, in which perhaps only Mr.
Maitland can rival him, Kovalevsky with wide command of
analogous facts and developments in Slavonic societies at
every stage of civilisation.   Mr. Kovalevsky derives the
Russian village community from the expansion of a patri-
archal family,[4] and calls attention to the fact that independent and dependent communities have actually existed in
Russia side by side in historical times.   This is of great
importance when equally universal and unqualified claims
are made on behalf of either type as the proximate original
of the English manor.

[1] It would be rather interesting to know when people began to
forget what it was, but this could be ascertained (save by good
luck) only with more labour than it would be worth.   In some
manors, e.g. Berkhamsted, name and thing had disappeared as
early as the reign of James I.

[2] Article on Mr. Vinogradoff's *Villainage in England, Law
Quart. Rev.*, viii. 117 ; and see "Early Forms of Landholding,"
Eng. Hist. Rev., i. 427.

[3] *Introduction to the History of the Law of Real Property*, 4th ed.
Oxford, 1892.

[4] *Modern Customs and Ancient Laws of Russia*, Lond. 1891
ch. iii.

I may add that the number and position of English land-holders who were certainly free at the time of the Domesday Survey, or at the date of King Edward's death, to which the Survey constantly refers, are among the elements to be most carefully considered in dealing with this problem of origins as a whole. That number was much underrated by Mr. Seebohm in consequence of his not allowing enough for the variety of Domesday terminology. The "theows" of Worcs., etc., are mostly not lords but rather small freeholders; and many tenants of the same class are entered merely by name. Thus the supposed "fact that Domesday does not mention free tenants in the greater part of England" (Mr. Ashley in *Econ. Rev.*, iii. 165) is an illusion.

With regard to the manorial courts, Mr. Maitland's researches (*Select Pleas in Manorial Courts*, published by the Selden Soc., 1888; and see Mr. G. H. Blakesley, "Manorial Jurisdiction," *Law Quart. Rev.*, v. 118) have proved, in my opinion, that the jurisdiction is feudal and derived from tenure, and independent alike of any earlier popular institutions and of economic organisation. The distinction between the "court baron" of the freeholders and the "customary court" of the base tenants is a relatively modern formalism; early medieval records know only of a *curia legalis* when there is any adjective at all. I now have no doubt that private jurisdiction is very ancient, and grew up not by transformation of any more ancient popular court, but in direct competition with the hundred court. There is no sufficient reason to think that there was ever any popular court less than the hundred court, and the "mark-moot," which students were for some time taught to believe in as if it were as well known as the King's Bench, is a creature of ingenious but unwarranted conjecture.

From all this it is a long and dangerous leap to the conclusion that the origin of our medieval land system is to any considerable extent not Germanic but Roman. I am no more disposed to accept any such conclusion myself than I was when I first wrote this book.

In 1893 Prof. Earle suggested in the *Economic Journal* that the syllable *wald* or *wel* in English place-names may

sometimes be a survival of a Roman *villa*. I know no
reason *a priori* why *villa* should not have survived sometimes,
as *castrum* certainly often did, but even if the evidence came
up to the mark of conviction, as I can hardly think it does,
I do not see that our general view of the history of civilisation in this island would be much affected.

Note D.—Villenage, Villein Tenure, and Copyholds

The first condition for a clear understanding of the "base
tenures" of our books is to keep in view the distinction
between the tenure of the land and the personal condition
of the tenant. For this, as recognised in the thirteenth
century, the classical authority is Bracton. He mentions
tenants on the king's demesne, whose ancestors held by free
services, but were put out by the strong hand, and were
allowed to take back their holdings to be holden in villenage
by base but certain and assigned services (cp. as to this *Dial.
de Scaccario*, I. c. x.). These tenants are personally free,
"since they perform their services not in regard of their
persons, but in regard of their holdings." Compare as to
this the old English document called *Rectitudines Singularum
Personarum*, § 2, p. 372, in Schmid's collection: the "cot-
setla," who renders labour-rent such as after the Conquest
was called servile, is personally free, for "he is to give his
hearth-penny on Holy Thursday as every free man ought";
so Kemble has well noted, *Saxons in England*, i. 323. To
return to the demesne tenants in Bracton, they cannot bring
the ordinary real actions, "but only the little writ of right
according to the custom of the manor"; that is, the jurisdiction was in the king, not as king, but as lord of the particular manor. Yet a tenant in ancient demesne might have
the assize of novel disseisin against a stranger, and under
exceptional conditions he or his feoffee might have it even
against the lord, see the opinion set out in Mr. Horwood's
Preface to Y. B., 20 & 21 Ed. I. p. xviii. They were called
glebae ascriptitii (cp. again the *Dial. de Scacc., loc. cit.*), but
Bracton regarded this as expressing not a bondage, but a
right; not that they might not go elsewhere, for "they shall

not be enforced to hold such a tenement unless they will," but that the lord cannot remove them as long as they perform the service (fo. 7a). Though not properly tenants in socage, they are regularly called common; cp. Old Nat. Brev. tit. "Briefe de recto clauso," fo. 11, ed. 1584. Again, "the tenement changes not the condition of a free man any more than of a slave. For a free man may hold in mere villenage, doing whatever service thereto belongs, and shall none the less be free, since he does this in regard of the villenage and not in regard of his person. . . . Mere villenage is a tenure rendering uncertain and unlimited services, where it cannot be known at eventide what service hath to be done in the morning, that is, where the tenant is bound to do whatever is commanded him" (Bracton, fo. 26a). Again, "another kind of tenement is villenage, whereof some is mere and other privileged. Mere villenage is that which is so held that the tenant in villenage, whether free or bond, shall do of villein service whatever is commanded him, and may not know at nightfall what he must do on the morrow, and shall ever be held to uncertain dues; and he may be taxed at the will of the lord for more or for less . . . yet so that if he be a free man he doth this in the name of villenage and not in the name of personal service . . . but if he be a villein [by blood], he shall do all these things in regard as well of the villenage as of his person" (fo. 208b). The only difference in the services was in the merchetum on marrying a daughter, which was an incident of personal servitude (being a fine paid to the lord for depriving him of a slave. As to the origin of the custom and word see Mr. Pike's Introduction to the Year-Book of 15 Edw. III. in the Rolls Series. I venture to guess that not only, as he suggests, the word has to do with mœor, and means a fine for marrying beyond the manor boundary, but the original form was mœor-scot, cp. the Domesday form circot = ciric-scot, which removes an otherwise serious objection: it occurs in Sussex, D. B. i. 29b, and in Oxfordshire (twice) 154b). Merchet was not of right demandable from the free man holding in villenage: "nec enim tenebitur ad merchetum de iure, quia hoc non pertinet ad personam liberi

r

sed villani"; and even on this point the evidence is not
uniform as in later books. Bracton's *de iure* suggests
doubt whether the practice was fixed in his own time.
Privileged villenage is then described as the tenure of the
personally free men already mentioned in the passage first
cited. Bracton also mentions a kind of qualified villenage
in which the services are defined by express agreement,
"ex conventione"; this is not properly called privileged,
but the terms agreed upon are enforceable against the lord
(fo. 209a). But I have some doubt whether these sentences
belong to the original text. I suppose the personally free
man who held in villenage, privileged or not, might always
perform the services by deputy if he could find one. Cp.
Bracton, fo. 199, 200, on the "exceptio villenagii," and
cases 70, 80, 281 in Bracton's *Note-Book*, ed. Maitland, 1887.

   Thus in Bracton it is quite clear that the conditions of
the tenure and the personal status of the tenant have no
necessary connection. Not only a free man may hold servile
land, but a bondman may hold and deal with free land as
against everybody but his own lord (fo. 26b), and he may in
general sue any one but his own lord, and in some cases
even him (155b); cp. Pollock and Maitland, *Hist. Eng. Law*,
i. 399. It is not uncommon for a group of unfree villeins
to find one man for particular works : this would usually be
one of themselves, but I doubt whether the lord cared who
did the work so long as it was done. And in Littleton,
and Coke's commentary on his text, the distinction is equally
clear (compare Co. Litt. 57b, 58a, with Litt. s. 172, and
Co. Litt. 116, 117). There is already a source of confusion,
however, in the double meaning of *villanus*. At the time
of Domesday the serf by blood was called *servus* (later
nativus), never *villanus*. But gradually, by a kind of
euphemism, the word *servus* was dropped, and *villanus* came
to mean sometimes, as aforetime, a man holding by a
certain kind of service, but often a man personally unfree.
In Glanvill we see the terminology in a state of transition.
He always calls the bondman *nativus*, but his condition (not
merely the tenure, but his personal state) is called *villenagium;* a reclaimed bondman is said to be *in villenagio*

positus, or in villenagium elementis. Bracton freely uses villanus as synonymous with nativus. By Littleton's time the word villein means, as a rule, to have imported personal servitude, though a careful man might speak of a " villein in blood " if he meant to secure himself against mistake. The distinction in substance, as above said, is still perfectly clear. Coke, perhaps, misinterprets Littleton in one place, s. 209. Littleton says that the lord of a manor cannot prescribe for a fine payable by every tenant within the manor who marries a daughter without the lord's license; "for none ought to make such fine but only villeins" Coke's gloss on this is as follows: " that is, either villeins of blood, or freemen holding in villenage or base tenure." Comparing Bracton's more explicit statement, it seems Littleton should have meant to exclude, not to include, freemen holding in villenage (s. 174, which suggests the contrary, and is cited by Coke, is not part of Littleton's own text, but an interpolation. See the note in Tomlins' edition, 1841). But Coke's view may be supported by Y. B. 10 Ed. III. 22, pl. 41, and 43 Ed. III. 5, pl. 13. And if he is wrong, it is only on a detail. When we come to Blackstone (Comm. II. 92-96) the confusion is complete. He writes as if wholly unaware that villanus ever meant anything but a personal serf: the liber homo tenens in villenagio somehow escapes his notice altogether, and the early copyholder is represented by him as an enfranchised bondman and nothing else. Blackstone's confused and misleading account has been adopted, so far as I know, by all modern text-writers before Mr. Kenelm Digby, who, going back to Littleton and Bracton, restored the distinction which Blackstone had obscured. The blundering of Blackstone's Commentaries on this point is the more remarkable, inasmuch as his Considerations on Copyholds show that he at one time read and to some extent appreciated the earlier authorities. Putting the tract and the Commentaries together, his theory, so far as he had one, appears to have been that personally free men holding in villenage existed, but were a very small class, and were ultimately represented by the customary tenants not said to hold at the will of the lord; that the

ordinary copyholder always represented a *nativus*; and that
the tenure of the *nativus* was not only burdensome, but
wholly precarious until long after the Conquest. This is
a long way from the facts, though perhaps not much further
than the opposite one of regarding the normal township as
a self-governing corporation, and villenage as a post-Norman
development or abuse of Anglo-Saxon serfdom.

As to the personal condition of the *nativi*, modern scholars
seem pretty well agreed that legally it might have been one
of great hardship, but in practice they were for the most
part not so very badly off. The least favourable view of
their position I have met with is Nasse's, the most favourable, Mr. Larking's (*Domesday of Kent*, note 57) and Mr.
Thorold Rogers's (*History of Prices*, vol. i.). These last writers
appear, however, at least as much concerned to make out the
state of the modern labourer worse as to make out the state
of the old *nativus* better. Mr. Thorold Rogers certainly
underrates the positive evidence that personal servitude, as
distinct from attachment to the soil, was known long after
the Conquest. For example, it was elaborately discussed in
1302 whether a neif marrying a free man became free
absolutely or only during the coverture (Y. B., 30 & 31
Ed. I. p. 164). Again, in 1305, it is pointedly stated by
the Court, the question being whether free or villein service
is due from certain land, that a plea of the tenant's personal
freedom is irrelevant as regards the land (Y. B., 33 Ed. I., p.
10). Probably it was not common for bondmen to be sold
apart from the land, but there is no doubt that it was sometimes done (Madox, *Form. Anglic.* Nos. 756-62). In the
absence of evidence it would be a plausible theory that the
ignorance or carelessness of Norman surveyors and judges
confused the lowest classes of free men with the bondmen,
in which process the dependent free man lost something, but
the bondman who formerly had no rights at all ultimately
gained much. Such a view has been taken by the Bishop of
Oxford (*Const. Hist.*, I. 429) and also by Mr. Freeman. But
the evidence shows a shifting (if anything) rather than a
confusion of the names, and possibly to some extent the
actual state, of different classes, a *Standesverschiebung* as one

might say in German. In the Exchequer Domesday we find on the manors of St. Paul's four distinct kinds of tenants, Villani, Bordarii, Cotarii, Servi. In the *Inquisitio of St. Paul's*, A.D. 1222, or in round numbers a century and a quarter later, we find Tenantes of several descriptions (libere tenentes, tenentes per villenagium, tenentes terras operarias, tenentes de terra assisa, and others), Cotarii, and Nativi. It may be difficult to assign the true relation of this classification to that of the Conqueror's surveyors (see *Rotation, Commons and Common Fields*, pp. 23 sqq.); but anyhow there is the fact that in the thirteenth century the minuter distinctions which the Conquest might be supposed to efface were as far from having disappeared as ever, and went on under changed or shifted names. It by no means follows, of course, that all these terms imply differences of personal status. It is hardly possible (especially after Mr. Seebohm's work) to maintain that *borderius* and *cotarius* signify anything but the general nature and size of the holding. But the leading types are well enough marked. In the eleventh century there was the free man in the fullest sense compatible with having a lord at all, who might "go where he would with his land," or, if he chose, alienate it, "vendere vel dare potuit," "potuit vendere cui voluit," in the phrase of Domesday Book. Then there was the dependent free man, who might seek a new lord if he chose, but at the cost of leaving the land: "potuit ire quo voluit, sed non cum terra." Such are the *coliberti* of Domesday in Dorset, elsewhere called "sokemen" (Eyton, p. 46),[1] and the thanes in the western counties who held church lands and "could not be separated from the church." Then we have the still more dependent holder (*ascriptitius* in the language of the twelfth-thirteenth century authorities, such as *Dial. Scacc.*, II. 14), who cannot quit the land without the lord's consent. Last of all comes the thrall or *servus*. In the thirteenth century,

---

[1] Eyton treats the *villani*, in Dorset at any rate, as an unfree class; but I fail to see why. Doubtless they were inferior to the *censarii*, who already paid a fixed money-rent for all service; but payment of labour-rents is quite compatible with personal freedom, otherwise no free man could ever have held in villenage.

I apprehend, these distinctions were by no means out of use, except that the power of seeking a new lord "cum terra sua" had disappeared, as being repugnant to feudal principles. The *liber homo, ascriptitius*, and *servus*, were still separate and defined conditions of men. The "ascriptitii qui villani dicuntur" of *Dial. Scacc.*, I. x., seem to be not serfs, but degraded free men. Again, we know that villenage by blood, as distinct from villein or customary tenure, existed and was recognised not only in books but in practice down to the seventeenth century. "Queen Elizabeth in 1574 issued a commission for the enfranchisement of most of the bond-servants in the manors belonging to the Crown. And there is a case reported 'as late as the fifteenth year of James I., in which an issue as to villenage was tried" (Elton, *Custom and Tenant-right*, p. 29). In the face of this it is impossible to hold that the sections of Littleton on villenage, for example, are the mere survival of legal pedantry describing obsolete institutions as if they were still alive.[1]

Thus much of the persons. Now for the tenure. It should really be needless at this day to contradict Blackstone's story that all our customary tenures were invented after the Conquest by the more or less capricious indulgence of the lords of manors. Still it may be worth while to re-capitulate the facts.

1. There is no reason whatever to suppose that the actual tillers of the land were materially disturbed by the Conquest, except where, as in Yorkshire, the land was harried as a punishment for stubborn resistance.[2]

2. Customary tenants are, in point of fact, found existing from Domesday till now without any discontinuous change in their tenure or its incidents : unless we are to count for

---

[1] As to the frequent and early commutation of services for money payment, see the Glastonbury Inquest, pp. 37, 69,100 ; in the two latter passages it appears as already of long standing. Even the distinction between fixed and arbitrary service as a test of the character of the holding is not always and absolutely to be relied on : see the Peterborough Book (Appendix to *Chron. Petrob.* Camd. Soc., 1849, p. 160), where we find sokemen bound for certain days in summer time to do "quidquid iusserit dominus."

[2] Cp. *Domesday of St Paul's*, Introd. p. xxx.

such the final allowance, temp. Ed. IV., of their right to
maintain their title in the King's courts even as against their
own lord.

3. The customs themselves bear every mark of archaic
origin. Transfer by symbolic ceremonies (which Blackstone
mentions in a sufficiently appropriate context, (bxxx. II. 313,
but without seeing its real significance) ; a variety of rules
of descent, showing affinities to early customs preserved in
other parts of Europe ; and the record and attestation of
title by the manorial courts, in forms apparently modelled
on ancient popular procedure ; all these things point not to
feudalism or to usages springing up under feudalism, but to
a state of society far older.

4. The country where common fields abound, as we learn
from the facts collected and discussed by Nasse, is also the
country of small copyholds. We know that common fields
represent a primitive system of agriculture. If copyhable
equally represent a primitive system of tenure, it is natural
that where the one persists the other should persist also.
If, as the account formerly received would have it, copyholds
are of post-Norman origin, the coincidence is inexplicable.

When Sir Edward Coke said that copyholders come of an
ancient house, he spoke more truth than he knew. The
ancient customary holders of land under a lord who were
not great men enough to hold their estates by charter before
the Conquest, and have them confiscated after it, are represented by the modern copyhold tenants, and in most cases
we may well think that the customary tenant practically
had a fixed tenure from the first. There is a significant
entry in the St. Paul's inquisition of 1222 (*Domesday of St.
Paul's*, ed. Hale, p. 52) : "Terre akermannorum quas dominus
potest capere in manu sua cum vult sine iniuriis hereditarie
successionis." The words as they stand might be clearer ;
but, "iniuriis" seems to stand for the more usual "calumpniis,"
i.e. claims, and the meaning to be that in these particular
holdings a deceased tenant's heir had not any customary
right to succeed. This implies that in other cases there was
such a customary right, especially when we bear in mind
the canon of inquiry that in medieval surveys what is un-

usual, not what is usual, is specially noted outside the common forms of description.

After all, there is no reason to suppose that the lawyers of Westminster in the thirteenth century were less dogmatic or more disposed to pay attention to the real facts and working of local usage than their followers in the sixteenth or nineteenth. Their confusion of *villanus* and *servus* may have been to some extent deliberate (Pollock and Maitland, *Hist. Eng. Law*, i. 413).

I do not say that in every case copyhold is an ancient customary holding. It is possible that servile tenements of the most precarious kind may, in the course of the Middle Ages, have grown to some extent into customary estates. Nay, I think there is one class of copyholds which may with considerable probability be referred to such an origin, the copyholds of so-called imperfect tenure which are still frequent in the western counties (Elton, *Custom and Tenant-right*, p. 63). These are the copyholds for lives or years where the fines are still uncertain, and there is no strict right of renewal,—a kind of estate which, in Mr. Elton's words, " by the severity of the lord's exactions, and the recurrence of a servile phraseology, is shown to have descended from the precarious holdings of the *natives* who could call nothing their own." Long as it has taken to establish even an inchoate tenant-right, I should be disposed to put back the origin of these holdings far beyond the Norman Conquest. They prevail only in the west of England, if indeed they are found at all elsewhere. There is no reason why this should be so if they began as the holdings of English serfs or degraded free men. But there is every reason why it should be so if they began as the holdings of a conquered British population who remained as the serfs and tenants at will of the English invaders on the land which had formerly been their own. In the east and south-east the British tillers of the soil were slain or dispersed. The remnant who may have been reduced to servitude left no distinct traces on the new form of society. In the west the English conquest was milder and more gradual. Still it was a conquest by the strong hand, and the relation of mere

sufferance which Blackstone imagined between the Norman
lord and the English customary tenant is like enough to
have really existed between the victorious English settler
and the Welshman who were the captives of his spear. It
seems a fair conjecture that the servile holdings of the West-
Welsh, little or not at all affected by the Norman Conquest,
have all these centuries been growing into what we now
know as copyholds of imperfect tenure.

In the case of the peculiar "conventionary" holdings of
the Cornish mining country, where the tenant has an inheritable interest, but must be readmitted every seven
years, something like proof of a Celtic origin is attainable.
This custom, fully described in Coxe's special report of
Rowe v. Brenton, presents distinct analogies to the customs
of Brittany.[1] Considering, again, the extreme antiquity of
tin mining in Britain, it seems at least probable that the
"tin-bounding" custom of Cornwall (and formerly of the
contiguous parts of Devon also), and the similar customs
which exist in the mining district of Derbyshire, come down
to us from a time earlier than the English occupation; and,
indeed, when we remember that in Cornwall the English
occupation is allowed to have been of the most superficial
kind, even by those who are least favourable to the preservation of Celtic elements elsewhere, there is hardly room for
two opinions on this point.

What is above suggested as to the origin of the imperfect
copyholds of the west of England may perhaps be strengthened
by consideration of the manner in which personal villenage
was distributed over the country at the date of the Domesday
survey. The Abstract of Population in the second volume
of Ellis's Introduction gives the facts ready to hand; and in
Mr. Seebohm's *English Village Community* they are exhibited
with the help of graphical charts (p. 86). We find that the
proportion of servi to the whole population steadily diminishes
as we go from the southern and western parts northward and
eastward. In Cornwall and Gloucestershire, the former still
really a West-Welsh county, the latter still half-Welsh, the

---

[1] *Coutumier Général*, iv. 409 (usances locales du domaine conque-
able de Cornouaille).

servi are almost one in four. In Devonshire they are little
short of one-fifth, in Shropshire over one-sixth, in Dorset
and Somerset not much under, and in Hampshire they are
over one-seventh ; in Worcestershire and Wiltshire it is
about the same.[1] As we cross from west to east there is a
notable change ; the average in the southern midlands, such
as Berks, Oxfordshire, Warwickshire, is roughly one-eighth.
As we go on to Leicestershire, Nottinghamshire, Stafford-
shire, Norfolk, and Suffolk, we find the serfs ten per cent of
the population at most. In Derbyshire there are hardly any
serfs, and in Lincolnshire, Huntingdonshire, Rutland, and
Yorkshire there are none at all. In the north-west, again,
Cheshire shows a small proportion, less than one-twelfth.
In the south-east the distribution seems irregular ; in Essex
the serfs are about one-ninth, in Kent something less than
one-tenth, in Surrey something more, while in Sussex they
are less than one-twentieth. Local accidents of forest and
fenland may in part account for these diversities ; the less
profitable soil would be more in servile occupation, and serfs
would be employed as herdsmen in the uncleared or half-
cleared forests. In any case the average is much below that
of the western counties. In one word, the serfs are fewer in
proportion as the English settlement of the country is more
complete. This decreasing ratio from west to east cannot be
an accident, and we are led to infer that both the descent
and the tenures of the *nativi* represented by the present
"imperfect copyholders" of the west were not English but
Welsh. Not that there is anything I know of to exclude
the possibility that the Welsh themselves before the English
invasion had serfs, who may not have been Celts or even
Aryans, or that these people left a permanent mark. Mr.
Elton (*Origins of English History*, ch. viii.) has collected a
mass of facts tending to show that the preference of younger
to elder sons, which in this country survives in the form of
borough-English, is derived from non-Aryan sources. And
ethnologists appear to be satisfied that the physical characters
of a prehistoric race of short and dark men who were

[1] In Herefordshire the proportion is evidently high, but the
numbers seem to be uncertain.

certainly neither Trutans nor Colts are amply visible in modern England. But for the present purpose I keep within historic limits.

How the king's courts came to assume, as they did at least as early as the beginning of the fourteenth century (Y. B., 30 & 31 Ed. I. 168), that there was no villenage in Kent is an unsolved riddle. The doctrine went so far that a man's freedom was established by showing that any of his ancestors was born in Kent, "quia ex impossibile servum procurare liberum" (Y. B., 33 Ed. 1. 15). But in Kent itself such was not the opinion or practice, for villenage certainly existed there much later, as Somner has shown (Treatise on Gavelkind, pp. 73-75); to say nothing of the difficulty of accounting for the total disappearance, within two centuries or thereabouts, of the servile class registered in Domesday. The legal doctrine, which no less certainly was acted upon by the courts out of Kent, is a curious example of the rapid growth and acceptance of fictions even when the facts contradicting them are not remote or difficult of access.

Note E.—Primogeniture in Socage Lands

There is still much obscurity about the manner in which primogeniture was extended from lands of military tenure to socage lands. It is certain that when Glanvill wrote—that is, about a century after the Conquest—gavelkind was still the prevailing rule. In Glanvill's chapter on inheritance (L. vii. c. 1) the rule of primogeniture, as a rule of common law, "secundum ius regni Angliae," is expressly confined to lands held by military service. As to the land of a "free soc-man," it has to be ascertained whether the land was partible by ancient custom. If so, the sons take equally, saving that the first-born has the chief dwelling-house, on the terms of making recompense in value to the others. If the land is not partible, then, "according to the custom of some, the first-born shall have the whole inheritance; according to the custom of others, however, the last-born son is heir." Thus primogeniture and borough-English appear as local customs on an equal footing. The best specific evidence of

customary primogeniture I know of is the case of certain
inferior tenants of the Prior of Canterbury, who were called
liberi sokmanni, but whose tenure had servile incidents (Elton,
Tenures of Kent, 106). It has been suggested that in this
case the rule was imposed after the Conquest on socagers who
were driven by need or the strong hand to accept grants in
base tenure (Kenny, *Essay on Primogeniture*, Cambridge,
1878, p. 31); but this, considering Glanvill's language,
appears by no means a safe inference. There are also local
rules of inheritance in various customary tenures, showing a
preference of the eldest (or sometimes the youngest) daughter.
(Elton, *Custom and Tenant-right*, Appendix D.) These evidently have nothing to do with feudalism. See further as to
customary primogeniture or indivisible holding Mr. (afterwards Sir R.) Morier's "Report on Tenure of Land in the
Grand Duchy of Hesse," Parl. Papers, 1870, lxvii. 193, 197.

In Bracton, writing after the lapse of nearly another
century, we find a significant difference, though not at first
sight a great one (fo. 76a). It is still a question in each case
whether the heritage is by ancient usage partible or not.
But if not, then primogeniture becomes the rule without
further inquiry. Local custom is to be considered only in the
case of villein tenure. Fleta (l. 5, c. 9, § 15) copies Bracton
almost word for word. Bracton's language shows the tendency
of primogeniture to increase, and the desire of lawyers to
hasten the process. We cannot accept it, however, as showing how far matters had really gone; and for this reason, that
it proves too much. What Bracton says does not admit of
the existence of borough-English in any land of freehold
tenure. But we know that there must have been borough-
English freeholds in Bracton's day; for there were such when
Littleton wrote, and there are still such in our own day.
Therefore, what we really learn from Bracton is that the
lawyers of the thirteenth century, in their zeal to improve
the position of primogeniture, were ready to outrun the
actual law and practice as they existed then and have existed
ever since.

Again, Bracton does not say or suggest that there was any
presumption for or against the partibility of socage lands.

Mr. Kenny (*Kenny on Primogeniture*, p. 20) has called attention to a case, decided in the year 1200, as showing that by
that time the burden of proof was on those who claimed
under the custom of division. The record is short enough to
quote in full (*Placita de term. S. Mich., 2 Joh., Abbrev.
Placit.* p. 29*b* ; since published from the original roll by the
Selden Society, *Select Civil Pleas*, vol. i. ed. W. P. Baildon,
1890, pl. 61) :—

" *Rutland.* Gilebertus de Betvill (petit) versus Willelmum
de Betvill duas virgatas terre cum pertinentiis in Cheureup
que sum (*sic*) contingunt de soagio, quod fuit patris eorum
in villa, et Willelmus venit et defendit ius eius et quod
soagium illud nunquam partitum fuit nec debet partiri et
hoc offert defendere per quendam liberum hominem suum.
[Gilbert offers two marks to the king to have an inquest
instead of trial by battle on the issue] utrum terra illa
partiri solet et sit partibilia. Et ipse voluit ponere se in
iuratam inde et quia Gilebertus nullam probam produxit
consideratum est quod Willelmus eat sine die et quietus."

This, however, does not show that there was a presumption in favour of primogeniture ; it only shows that there
was no presumption to the contrary. The holding might or
might not be divisible by ancient custom ; whether it was so
was a question of fact. It was the plaintiff's business, as in
any other case, to prove the facts on which he relied, and
among them that the land had from ancient times been divisible. Failing to prove this, he lost his cause. It does not
appear that if the elder son had been plaintiff he would not
in like manner have been called on to prove that primogeniture was the local rule.

It is certain, however, that during the thirteenth century
primogeniture made great advances. Before the century was
out it had come to be spoken of as the common law of
England. In 1292 we find it said that " in some places as
well the tenements holden in socage as other tenements are
governed by the common law " ; and the custom of Kent is
already spoken of as peculiar (Y. B. 20 Ed. I. in Record
Office Series, pp. 327, 329) : but then, and some years later,
it was still an open question of fact whether given socage lands

were partible or not (30 Ed. I. p. 50, A.D. 1302). There
came a time, no doubt, and probably not long after this, when
by making the rules of evidence more stringent the partible
tenure, except in Kent, was extinguished. But specific evidence of the steps by which the process was completed appears
to me to be still wanting.

NOTE F.—"CESTUI QUE USE" AT COMMON LAW

The action of *assumpsit* was about contemporaneous with
the doctrine of uses in its introduction and development : it
became at last the common method of enforcing simple contracts, but originally was not an action on the promise itself,
but on the breach of a duty incident to the promise, a "tort
founded in contract," as the modern phrase runs. The object,
in fact, was to get a remedy where the contract itself could
not be sued on in any of the recognised forms of action. I
do not know what there was to prevent the judges, if they
had chosen, from holding that a conveyance to uses created a
duty in the feoffees which would support an action of *assumpsit* in case of breach or neglect. Again, they might well
enough have given *cestui que use* an action of account for the
profits, or an action on the case analogous to it. Neither
of these remedies, however, would have been anything like so
effectual as the Chancellor's decrees.

Bacon's summary of the mischiefs aimed at by the statute
is worth citing. (*Works*, ed. Spedding, vii. 418.) "The particular inconveniences by the law rehearsed may be reduced
to four heads : first, that these conveyances in use are weak
for consideration " (*i.e.* made without fitting deliberation) ;
"secondly, that they are obscure and doubtful for trial ;
thirdly, that they are dangerous for want of notice and publication ; fourthly, that they are exempted from all such
titles as the law subjecteth possession unto."

Notwithstanding the dislike of the common lawyers to
uses, the sages of the law did not scruple to employ them for
their own convenience. Littleton had lands in use, and in
1481 disposed of the use by his will (see it set out in the

notes to his life in Tomline's edition of his Timaeus, 1841, p. xxxiv.)

Note G.—Settlements and Property

Estates for life, followed by one or more estates tail in remainder, were a known form of disposition as early as the fourteenth century. In the Calendar of Patent Rolls for 7 Ed. II. (p. 76, ed. 1802) this grant occurs :—

" Rex confirmavit Ricardo de Pymelmdon pro vita, rem' diversis filiis suis in generali tallio omnia sua hereditamenta in Worthynbury in partibus de Mayloreysmaalis per servic' quartae partis unius feodi milit'."

On the next page is a grant of successive estates tail without a preceding life estate :—

" Rex confirmavit Johanni de Kllerker in generali tallio rem' aliis in generali tallio cert' haeredit' in Kllerker ei dat' per Episcopum Dunolm' [sic] pro annuo reddit' 3s. 9d."

In the later time of Edward I. there appear several grants in tail, often to a man and his wife, and sometimes there is a remainder in fee-simple (ib. p. 51, col. 2 at foot) ; but for the most part the grants abstracted are in fee-simple.

The history of the further development of settlements was traced by the late Mr. Joshua Williams (*Transactions of the Juridical Society*, i. 45). He states, as the result of a careful examination of documents preserved in the MS. collections of the British Museum, that limitations in substantially the modern form to the use of a man for life, remainder to his first and other sons in tail, were not uncommon in the latter part of the sixteenth century ; the parties being content apparently to take the risk of the contingent remainders being destroyed by the feoffment (or other act amounting to a discontinuance), or forfeiture by waste, etc., of the tenant for life. The introduction of trustees to preserve contingent remainders in order to meet this risk is ascribed by a professional tradition, which was established by the middle of the last century (Blackstone, *Comm.* II. 172 ; cp. Lord Hardwick in Garth v. Cotton, 1 Dick. 188, 191, and the argu-

ments of the same case, 1 Ves. Sr. 524, 548), to Orlando
Bridgman and Geffrey Palmer, whose invention, it is suggested, was sharpened by the troubles of the Civil Wars to
the better securing of their clients' estates.

In Orlando Bridgman's *Precedents of Conveyances* the
limitation to a trustee, after the determination of the tenant
for life's estate, and during his natural life, "upon trust
only for preserving the contingent uses and estates herein-
after limited, and to make entries for the same if it shall be
needful," appears in regular use (though sometimes it is
omitted), and in that form it does not appear to occur earlier.
Limitations curiously similar in form, though differing from
this in substance, as careful examination will show, were,
however, in use nearly a century before. In Holcroft's case,
Moore, 486, we find an estate settled by fine in the second
year of Mary (1554-55) to the use of Sir John Holcroft the
younger for life " so long and until he attempt to alien, and
then to the use of Hamlet [Holcroft], and the heirs males of
his body during the life of Sir John the younger ; and immediately after his death " remainders to the first and other
sons of Sir John the younger in tail male, down to the fourth
son inclusive, remainder to Hamlet Holcroft in tail male, remainders over. The estate limited to Hamlet during Sir
John's life comes exactly in the place where, in Bridgman's
and later settlements, the estate of the trustees to preserve
contingent remainders would come. But, for whatever purpose it was inserted, it cannot well have been to preserve the
remainders to Sir John's unborn sons ; for supposing that no
son was in existence when Hamlet entered upon Sir John's
attempt to alien (and assuming, which is not clear, that the
"attempt to alien " refers to a tortious conveyance of the fee,
and not merely to alienation of the life estate), then Hamlet's
estate tail *pur auter vie* and his remoter estate tail in remainder would coalesce and shut out the intermediate contingent remainders. It seems to have been intended merely
as a check on the tenant for life. Only one step, however, was
needed to make an estate of this kind a protection for the
remainders as well, and that step was taken by Bridgman and
Palmer when they limited it to a trustee specially appointed

for the purpose, and with an express declaration of the trust. Modern conveyancing as a whole, and the regular use of settlements in their modern form, certainly date from about Bridgman's time. A brief but clear and admirably written account of the elements of the subject, both doctrinal and historical, is given in the part of Blackstone's Commentaries, already referred to (Book II. ch. ii.); it might be needless to mention this, but the text of Blackstone is nowadays unduly neglected, partly by reason of exaggerated criticisms which have obtained currency, partly from the ravages it has suffered at the hands of so-called editors. Advanced students will of course consult the late Mr. Davidson's exhaustive Introduction to his volume on Settlements.

As to the history of the rule against perpetuities, the following dates may be not without curiosity for readers of this note:—

1681-83. Duke of Norfolk's case (3 Ca. Ch.) Limitations to take effect within lives in being held good, and an attempted distinction between terms of years and freehold interests rejected.

1697. Lloyd v. Carew (Pre. Ch. 72, 106, and Shower, Ca. Parl. 137). Twelve months after lives in being, good.

1699. Scattergood v. Edge, 12 Mod. 287. Still doubtful whether a life or lives in being were not the extreme limit: "It was a great policy of the common law that alienations should be encouraged; for it is the greatest preserver and promoter of industry, trade, arms, and stunly: and this was visible from the making of the statute *De Donis*, until common recoveries were found out; and these executory devises had not been long countenanced when the judges repented them, and if it were to be done again, it would never prevail; and therefore there are bounds set to them, viz. a life or lives in being; and further they shall never go by my consent, let Chancery do as they please*: per Treby, C. J.

1736. Stephens v. Stephens. (Ca. temp. Talbot, 228.) Executory devise to an unborn child of a living person when he shall attain the age of twenty-one years held good. This was the conclusive decision.

Q

1765. Blackstone. (*Comm.* II. 174.) "The utmost length that has been hitherto allowed for the contingency of an executory devise of either kind to happen in, is that of a life or lives in being, and one-and-twenty years afterwards."

1787. Jee *v.* Audley, 1 Cox, 324, 1 Rev. Rep. 46. (Sir Lloyd Kenyon, M. R.) The rule considered to be settled : "it is grown reverend by age, and is not now to be broken in upon."

1833. Cadell *v.* Palmer, in House of Lords, 1 Cl. & F. 372. The term not exceeding twenty-one years which may be added to lives in being is a term in gross, *i.e.* it need not have reference to any minority.

A very full history of the doctrine is contained in Hargrave's argument in Thellusson *v.* Woodford, 4 Ves. 247 *sqq.* (also separately printed in his *Juridical Arguments,* vol. ii.), and Sir E. Sugden's in Cadell *v.* Palmer.

The allowance of the period of gestation when gestation exists (but not as a term in gross of nine or ten months) is properly treated by the best writers on the subject as being not a special clause or part of this rule, but an application of the general principle that an unborn child is treated, when-ever it will be for his benefit, as being actually in existence ; and I have so stated it in the text. It is now judicially settled, after much difference of opinion, that remainders are also subject to another rule which is not merely a particular example of the rule against perpetuities, namely, that an estate cannot be limited to any child or issue (as purchasers) of a person not in existence : Whitby *v.* Mitchell (1890) 44 Ch. Div. 85. Much might be said about the history of the doctrine, but this is hardly the place for it. The learned reader may consult Williams on *Real Property,* 17th ed. p. 380, and the preface to vol. viii. of the *Revised Reports.*

A question in some measure connected with the doctrine of perpetuity is how far there can exist at common law a fee-simple determinable otherwise than by failure of heirs, or by the re-entry of the grantor or his heirs for a condition broken. To put the question in a concrete instance : apart from the Statute of Uses, and apart from any question of perpetuity, is a grant good in this form : To J. S. and his

heirs as long as Lincoln's Inn Hall, or as a certain tree,
shall stand? Plowden thought such a grant was good, and
operated by way of limitation, not condition (which distinction
must be carefully observed) : Plowden, 557, cp. Scholastica's
case, ib. 414. And Coke in Seymor's case (10 Rep. 97b)
says there is a fee-simple determinable by limitation, as
distinguished from one determinable by condition ; "as if A
enfeoff B of the manor of D to have and to hold to him
and his heirs, so long as C has heirs of his body, and that is
called a fee-simple limited and qualified." No remainder or
reversion can be expectant on it. There is also a fee-simple
determinable "implicit, and derived out of an estate tail,"
which is known as a base fee ; its nature is comparatively
common learning. In Liford's case (11 Rep. 49a) we read
that "a man may have an inheritance in fee-simple in lands,
as long as such a tree shall grow, because a man may have
an inheritance in the tree itself." But this appears to be
said only in the course of argument. The Year-Book referred
to (27 Hen. VIII. 29b) gives the fanciful reason that an estate
may as well depend on the life of a tree as of a man. This
also appears to be extra-judicial. Neither the reason in
Coke's report nor that in the Year-Book can be said to
strengthen the proposition.

On the other hand, Coke's contemporary Anderson, Chief
Justice of the Common Pleas, appears to have been of the
contrary opinion ; according to what is given in his reports
(2. 138, 139) as the resolution of the Court in Corbet's case,
the only determinable fee-simple (not upon condition) known
to the law is a base fee, as, when a villein is tenant in tail,
and his lord enters on him, or tenant in tail is attainted of
high treason, the lord or the Crown has a fee-simple determinable on the failure of issue inheritable under the gift in
tail : he seems to think parties cannot make a gift in fee-
simple determinable in any other way than by entry for
condition broken, which is a different matter. The cases
and opinions in the Year-Books referred to in Anderson are
partly unverifiable by reason of wrong or misprinted references, partly not to the point, being concerned with conditions against alienation by a tenant in tail, and in one place

(13 H. VII. 24) there is an unresolved difference of opinion. If there bo a feoffment in fee for "so long as J. S. has issue," it is asserted on the one part and denied on the other that the "condition" (but a condition in the proper sense can hardly be meant) is void ; the reporter adds "ideo quaere." Modern writers are not agreed either. Some, and notably Mr. Challis, following Preston, are confident that such estates can exist, some that they cannot.

On the whole, it appears that the point has never been settled. I cannot help thinking that the silence of Coke's commentary on Littleton (where surely he would have explained the nature of such estates, and distinguished them from estates upon condition, had he deliberately allowed them : see especially 214b) weighs much against the dicta in his reports. Also it is strange that Littleton himself (ss. 380, 381, etc.) had nothing to say of such estates, if in his time they were known to the law. It may be that after the statute *De Donis* an estate to A and his heirs as long as B shall have heirs of his body (as put in Seymor's case) was exceptionally allowed, or thought allowable, by analogy to a base fee.

If a fee-simple determinable on an arbitrary event is a possible estate at common law, it seems to be not within the rule against perpetuities. It also seems probable that since the statute of *Quia emptores* the possibility of reverter would belong not to the grantor or his heirs, but to the chief lord of the fee. Whether such possibility (if any such there can be) is a "possibility coupled with an interest" within 8 & 9 Vict. c. 106, s. 6, so that it may now be disposed of by deed, is a point that may be considered at leisure by the curious.

The learned reader is further referred to the remarks of Prof. J. C. Gray, of Harvard University, and Mr. H. W. Challis on Determinable Fees in the *Law Quarterly Review*, iii. 399, 403.

NOTE H

The law relating to the settlement and transfer of land, and various proposals for its amendment, are considered in the following recent publications :—

Land Transfer. Published by order of the Bar Committee. London: Butterworths, 1886. Cp. Law Quarterly Review, ii. 307.

Statement on the Land Laws. By the Council of the Incorporated Law Society of the United Kingdom. London: Butterworths, 1886. Cp. the articles cited below.

On the Transfer of Land. By H. W. Elphinstone. In Law Quarterly Review, 1886, ii. 12. At p. 237 of the same volume the same writer gives a concise critical account of a number of tracts and articles on the subject, of which the titles are there collected.

The Council of the Incorporated Law Society on the Land Laws. Articles in the Solicitors' Journal, 1886, January 30 to March 6 inclusive.

Registration of title to land, and how to establish it without cost or compulsion. By Charles Fortescue-Brickdale. London: E. Stanford, 1886. Cp. Law Quarterly Review, iii. 86.

The Land Transfer Bill. Solicitor's Journal, April 9, 16, 1887. The second article gives a list of publications, including documents on the Torrens system in the Australian Colonies.

Transfer of Land by Registration of Title. By T. B. Colquhoun Dill. London: Cassell and Co., 1893.

Notes on Land Transfer in various Countries. By Charles Fortescue-Brickdale. London: Law Times Office, 1894.

INDEX

www.ingramcontent.com/pod-product-compliance
Lightning Source LLC
Chambersburg PA
CBHW030407270326
41926CB00009B/1310